Contents

List of tables	iv
About the authors	v
Acknowledgements	vi
Summary	vii
Introduction and policy background	1
Changing the policy climate: liberating the NHS	3
Defining accountability	7
Current and future accountability relationships for commissioners and providers	10
Commissioners	10
Providers	19
Will the new accountability system meet the government's policy aims?	31
Is this the end of performance management and central control?	31
Will the health service be more locally accountable?	33
Do the reforms create a more level playing field for providers?	37
Will publishing performance information make the service more accountable?	39
Will the system be fit for purpose?	41
Is the system coherent?	41
Does it target the right actors?	42
What will accountability relationships be like in practice?	43
Conclusions	45
References	49

List of tables

Table 1 Current accountability relationships for commissioners of NHS care 18

Table 2 Future accountability relationships for commissioners of NHS care 18

Table 3 Current accountability relationships for providers of NHS hospital care 26

Table 4 Future accountability relationships for providers of NHS hospital care 26

Table 5 Current accountability relationships for general practices 29

Table 6 Future accountability relationships for general practices 29

ACCOUNTABILITY IN THE NHS
Implications of the government's reform programme

Jo Maybin, Rachael Addicott, Anna Dixon, John Storey

Published by

The King's Fund

11–13 Cavendish Square

London W1G 0AN

Tel: 020 7307 2568

Fax: 020 7307 2801

www.kingsfund.org.uk

© The King's Fund 2011

First published 2011 by The King's Fund

Charity registration number: 1126980

ISBN: 978 1 85717 617 9

A catalogue record for this publication is available from the British Library

Available from:

The King's Fund

11–13 Cavendish Square

London W1G 0AN

Tel: 020 7307 2568

Fax: 020 7307 2801

Email: publications@kingsfund.org.uk

www.kingsfund.org.uk/publications

Edited by Fiona Weston

Typeset by Peter Powell Origination & Print Ltd

Printed in the UK by The King's Fund

About the authors

Jo Maybin

Jo Maybin is a Senior Researcher at The King's Fund, where she conducts research and analysis on contemporary NHS policy developments. In 2010 she co-edited a major review of NHS performance under the last Labour government. She holds a Sir Bernard Crick Fellowship in politics from the University of Edinburgh, where she is working part-time on a PhD that explores how national policy-makers in health use knowledge. Prior to joining The King's Fund in 2006, Jo worked as a social affairs analyst in BBC News. She has a degree in social and political sciences from Cambridge, and an MSc in political theory from the LSE.

Rachael Addicott

Rachael Addicott has been a Senior Research Fellow at The King's Fund since 2007, having previously been a Lecturer in Public Sector Management at Royal Holloway University of London. Rachael has an interest in organisational change and models of governance and accountability in the public sector. She works on a number of projects in these areas, including foundation trusts, employee ownership and networks. Rachael has a PhD in health service management from Imperial College London and will in 2011/12 be a Commonwealth Fund Harkness Fellow.

Anna Dixon

Anna Dixon is Director of Policy at The King's Fund. She has conducted research and published widely on health care funding and policy. She has given lectures on a range of topics including UK health system reform and patient choice. She was previously a lecturer in European Health Policy at the London School of Economics and was awarded the Commonwealth Fund Harkness Fellowship in Health Care Policy in 2005/6. Anna has also worked in the Strategy Unit at the Department of Health, where she focused on a range of issues including choice, global health and public health.

John Storey

John Storey is Professor of Management at the Open University Business School. He is lead author of *Governing the New NHS: Issues and tensions in health service management* (Routledge 2011). He is Principal Investigator for the ongoing NIHR/SDO project on the role of clinical leadership in service redesign and was Principal Investigator for the recently completed NIHR/SDO project on the intended and unintended consequences of governance arrangements in the NHS.

Acknowledgements

We would like to thank Arturo Alvarez-Rosete and Tony Harrison and our colleagues at The King's Fund for their input and feedback on earlier versions of this paper. Rudolf Klein and Chris Ham provided very helpful review comments, and we are grateful as ever to Mary Jean Pritchard for her editorial input. Any errors or omissions are our own.

Summary

The Health and Social Care Bill sets out a radical series of reforms for the National Health Service (NHS) in England, and represents a significant attempt to reduce the day-to-day involvement that politicians, civil servants and managers will have in health care.

This paper gives an overview of how providers and commissioners of NHS-funded care are currently held to account, and considers how this would change under the government's reform programme. At the time of writing, the Bill is still making its way through parliament and has been subject to strong criticism. Whether the Bill will be passed in the form we describe here is uncertain; the issues raised in this paper should contribute to the current debate.

We define accountability as the requirement for organisations to report and explain their performance, and we distinguish between 'soft' and 'hard' accountability, with the latter involving the possibility of sanctions if the account-giver is not able to satisfy the account-holder (Klein and New 1998). We identify five main types of accountability relationship, which we label as accountability by:

- scrutiny (for example, of NHS trusts by local overview and scrutiny committees)

- management (for example, of primary care trusts by strategic health authorities)

- regulation (for example, of secondary care providers by the Care Quality Commission)

- contract (such as relationships between commissioners and providers)

- election (such as the appointment of foundation trust governors by the trust members).

For commissioners of NHS care, the government claims that the reforms will mean a shift away from top-down performance management relationships as the principal lever for accountability towards a stronger reliance on regulation and local scrutiny. However, we identify the strong potential for relationships between the consortia of GPs and their practice teams (GP consortia) and the NHS Commissioning Board, and between both organisations and the Secretary of State, to resemble command-and-control managerial relationships in practice. Although the government is proposing to relinquish its powers of general direction over the service, it will nonetheless retain strong and potentially broad powers in relation to commissioners.

The potential weakness of both GP consortia's internal governance mechanisms and the role of health and wellbeing boards means that the NHS Commissioning Board and the Secretary of State may well have good reason to intervene.

If the government wants to move away from a service characterised by strong performance management by government and other agencies, GP commissioning consortia must be mandated and supported to develop strong internal governance mechanisms to reduce the need for such intervention. These requirements should be set out as a matter of urgency, as pathfinder consortia are already establishing their organisational forms.

The powers of health and wellbeing boards should also be strengthened. While we do not think these boards should have a hierarchical hold over commissioning consortia, we do think their role could be strengthened by requiring the NHS Commissioning Board's assessment of consortia to consider their views.

Providers of NHS-funded care are currently subject to quite different accountability relationships depending on whether they provide primary or secondary care, and, in the secondary care sector, on the nature of their ownership and governance status. The reforms will see GP practices (as providers) subject to a host of new accountability requirements, bringing them closer into line with their secondary care counterparts. These new demands will prove particularly challenging for small and single-handed practices.

For secondary care providers, the reforms will mean a harmonisation of the accountability requirements for foundation trusts, independent providers and third-sector providers (though foundation trusts will have an additional legal requirement to have governance relationships involving patient, public and/or staff representation). For NHS providers, especially those that don't currently have foundation trust status, the changes will mean a significant shift away from performance management towards a reliance on regulation, contracts and internal governance arrangements supplemented by local scrutiny arrangements.

There are grounds for pessimism about the likely scale of the impact on providers of changes to local accountability mechanisms. On the basis of evaluations of foundation trust governance arrangements to date, we query whether their extension to the rest of the hospital sector will have any immediate and significant impact on the extent to which these organisations feel accountable to the local population. The role of trust boards in improving quality will take on a new significance, and these bodies will need to be supported and strengthened if they are to fulfil this task. Financial pressures on local authorities may also squeeze an already under-resourced scrutiny function. Further, regulation is often excluded from traditional definitions of accountability as it focuses only on compliance with minimum standards. Thus, how far providers will be accountable for delivering a good or excellent service will depend heavily on the role played by commissioners (through contracts), whose effectiveness is likely to vary considerably at a local level. As things stand, the potential for the accountability of secondary care providers to be underpowered is a major cause for concern.

However, we also emphasise that the reality of an accountability regime is usually determined by how relationships play out in practice – which in turn tends to be shaped by the pre-existing values and behaviour of organisations, and by the perceptions and power of relevant actors, those at the top of key organisations such as the NHS Commissioning Board, Monitor and the Care Quality Commission, as well as on the views and behaviour of the Secretary of State.

Overall, we think the proposed reforms signal a shift to an over-reliance on weak and unproven accountability relationships given the extent of the government's proposed reforms; this is a significant cause for concern. Given that the NHS remains one of the largest domains of public expenditure, and that there are increasing pressures on budgets in the current tighter fiscal climate, there will continue to be demands for political accountability, both for how the money is being spent and for how local services are provided, particularly where there are closures. The dismantling of lines of managerial and political accountability might make it more difficult for elected politicians in Westminster to get a clear account in future, but they will no doubt try. Systems of contractual accountability and oversight by local democratic bodies may not be sufficient to satisfy their demands. Whatever the government's intentions, we may, in practice, see pressure to a return to central managerial and political accountability for providers as well as commissioners of NHS care.

Introduction and policy background

The Health and Social Care Bill (House of Commons Bill 2010–11) sets out a potentially radical series of reforms for the NHS in England that will redefine the way that central government and politicians interact with frontline commissioning and provision of care. These reforms – before parliament at the time of writing – represent a major attempt to increase local democratic accountability and reduce the day-to-day involvement that politicians, civil servants and managers have in the health care system.

They symbolise a significant shift in the way that those involved in planning, delivering and commissioning care are held to account, and by whom, with the changes in these relationships being reflected in:

■ who is holding whom to account (the account holders)

■ the number and strength of the lines of accountability (for the account giver)

■ the mechanisms of accountability.

For some organisations and professional groups involved in commissioning and delivering health care, these shifts in accountability represent a significant change in how they relate to different parts of the system and the level of scrutiny they are under.

The abolition of existing account holders (such as strategic health authorities and primary care trusts), the creation of new organisational forms (such as the NHS Commissioning Board and GP commissioning consortia), and the elevated role for other groups (such as local authorities and Monitor) will create a new accountability landscape for the service. Given their speed and far-reaching nature, it is imperative that there is clarity about the impact these reforms will have on how the system will be held to account.

This paper provides an overview of current and future accountability relationships for commissioners and providers of NHS care – how accountability operates in the NHS today, and how accountability might operate following the reforms. It draws particular attention to the more significant and revolutionary changes in how commissioners and providers will be held to account under the reforms proposed in the Bill.

There are a number of caveats with regard to the analysis that follows.

First, this paper deliberately focuses on the providers and commissioners of health care and their most direct organisational accountability links. As such, although we consider some onward accountability relationships (such as those to the Secretary of State), a more comprehensive description of the broader accountability landscape – such as the links between politicians and parliament – is beyond the scope of this paper.

Second, this paper provides an analysis at the organisational level – focusing on organisations and relationships that cover whole-system accountability for all kinds of care. A report by the NHS Confederation and Independent Healthcare Advisory Services (2009) found that NHS and independent sector health care providers were collectively subject to overview by some 35 regulatory, auditing, inspectorate and accreditation agencies. For the sake of clarity about the most significant changes, we do not consider professional regulation or regulation through the host of more specific regulatory bodies, such as the Human Fertilisation and Embryology Authority and the Human Tissue Authority.

Third, we have not included an analysis of public health reform in this discussion. Public health in England is organised differently from other health care provision, and involves a distinct set of actors and relationships. At the time of writing, the organisation and provision of public health in England is undergoing a separate reform process and is at an earlier stage of restructure (*see* Department of Health 2010b). Because of these differences, accountability in public health is clearly worthy of scrutiny. However, that is beyond the scope of this paper.

Finally, for practical purposes, the paper assumes that the reforms will be implemented in full, although at the time of writing the Bill is still making its way through parliament and has been subject to strong criticism. Whether it will be passed in the form we describe here is therefore not a foregone conclusion; the issues raised in this paper should contribute to the current debate.

We begin by defining what we mean by accountability and how variations in the mechanisms of accountability may be defined in practice. We discuss how the organisational and structural changes to the NHS proposed by the coalition government are likely to impact on accountability, that is, the way in which organisations within the NHS are held to account for the way they spend public money. The paper will then go on to discuss whether these reforms are likely actually to achieve the government's stated objectives of a more locally accountable system, free of central government control and performance management. Using evidence from elements of these reforms introduced by the previous government, this paper will consider whether the proposed changes to accountability are likely to be as far-reaching and radical as they appear.

We begin with a brief overview of some of the more significant elements of the reform. Later sections will consider how these reforms specifically affect the changing nature of accountability.

Changing the policy climate: liberating the NHS

The NHS experienced a period of intense organisational and structural change under the previous government, which, from 2000, attempted to shift the balance of decision-making power away from central government to local NHS organisations (both providers and commissioners), independent regulators and arm's length bodies, and patients and the public. These reforms were intended to weaken the link between ministers and the day-to-day operation of the NHS.

As part of these reforms, the Labour government created new organisations – including, for example, the semi-autonomous foundation trusts for acute care and mental health provider organisations, new commissioning bodies (the reconfigured primary care trusts), a new independent regulator (Monitor) for the foundation trusts, and a new Care Quality Commission. That government also introduced new mechanisms by which the public could have a stronger voice in shaping the services the NHS provides. However, in practice, the Labour government's earlier emphasis on strong and centralised performance management continued to have a significant grip on the service throughout its administration, and these two different approaches to holding the service to account came to exist in parallel (Addicott 2005; Exworthy *et al* 2009; Storey *et al* 2010).

In 2010, the Conservative–Liberal Democrat coalition's programme for government set out a number of proposals consonant with the Labour government's reforms: decentralisation, increased local accountability and autonomy, and reduced central control. The coalition government's stated ambition is 'to free NHS staff from political micromanagement, increase democratic participation in the NHS and make the NHS more accountable to the patients that it serves' (Her Majesty's Government 2010, p 24).

These proposals aimed to redefine the relationship between government and the NHS, as well those between various organisations within the NHS. Following publication of a White Paper and several consultations on particular changes, these reforms have been embodied in the Health and Social Care Bill (House of Commons Bill 2010–11), which is currently before parliament.

The overarching ethos of the reform agenda is for a smaller government bureaucracy and a freeing up of the day-to-day operation of the health service from central political control. The declared intentions of the reforms are to grant commissioners and providers greater autonomy and flexibility over decision-making and to give patients greater involvement in decisions affecting their care. This is part of the government's localism and so-called Big Society agendas, to shift decision-making responsibilities to local communities and move away from large, state-run monopolies. Key aspects of the government's reform agenda that

are pertinent to the discussion of accountability presented here are summarised in
the box.

**Summary of key aspects of system reform proposed in the Health and
Social Care Bill**

Commissioners and strategic health authorities

Primary care trusts are to be abolished, and the majority of their
commissioning responsibilities will be held by consortia of GP practices.
Under the government proposals, all GP practices will be required to become
members of a GP consortium that will hold real budgets and commission
the majority of NHS services for its patients (including elective hospital
care, rehabilitative care, urgent and emergency care, most community health
services, and mental health and learning disability services). The NHS
Commissioning Board will hold GP consortia to account for quality standards
and patient outcomes, and will retain responsibility for commissioning some
services, including primary care and some specialised services.

Strategic health authorities will be abolished completely. The coalition has also
agreed to reduce the number of regulators and so-called quangos, such as the
Audit Commission.

Provider autonomy and diversity

There is a commitment to give providers more autonomy, reflected in the
directive that all trusts are to become foundation trusts by April 2014. This
reform reflects the previous administration's intention. Originally, all trusts
were to become foundation trusts by December 2008, but that date was
subsequently revised and ultimately missed (Exworthy *et al* 2009). Some
trusts have continued to struggle to reach the standard required to become
a foundation trust. The coalition government has established an NHS Trust
Development Authority to assist with the transition.

In future, failing providers will largely be dealt with by the market, that is they
will be taken over by other organisations (including the private sector) or put
into administration. The economic regulator Monitor (see below) will have
powers to ensure continuity of essential services at a local level while the Care
Quality Commission (CQC) continues to have the authority to fine or suspend
services that fail to meet its essential safety and quality requirements. This
authority will apply to all providers of NHS health and social care, including
private organisations and third sector providers.

To generate greater competition and remove some of the barriers to entry for new providers, services will be commissioned from 'any qualified provider'. The intention of opening up the market to any provider is to allow patients greater choice, and is guided by the idea that competition will stimulate innovation and improvements, and increase productivity.

The coalition government aims to create the 'largest and most vibrant social enterprise sector in the world' (Department of Health 2010a, p 36), particularly through extending the freedoms of foundation trusts. There will be greater flexibility to allow 'spin-offs' from foundation trusts, in which particular clinical areas can be established as social enterprises providing services to the foundation trust.

A new role for Monitor

Under the government's proposals, Monitor will become an economic regulator for all providers of NHS services, jointly responsible with the CQC for licensing providers. Monitor will promote competition where appropriate, set prices, and secure the continuation of 'designated' (or essential) services (House of Commons 2010–11). This new role may represent one of the most significant innovations among these reforms, being a key component of 'the most ambitious attempt yet seen to apply a system of market regulation to the NHS' (Ham 2011).

Monitor will be charged with ensuring that all providers act within competition law, that they meet information reporting requirements, and that continued access to 'designated' services is maintained. It will have the power to set special licence conditions in circumstances such as:

- if a provider enjoys a particular position of 'market power' within its local area, or if there is a need to protect service continuity

- to trigger a special administration regime in cases of service failure

- to protect assets or facilities

- to require monopoly providers to grant access to their facilities to third parties

- to issue fines

- to suspend or revoke a provider's license.

A greater role for local authorities

The government proposes that local authorities will take on responsibility for leading public health and health improvement at a local level, and that new health and wellbeing boards will be established in upper tier authorities – eg, county council and unitary authorities. These boards would have two main functions: assessing the health needs of their local population and co-ordinating and integrating the commissioning of health and social care services. These proposals signal the intention to integrate further the planning for health improvement activities with those of other service areas, such as transport, housing and leisure, in order to tackle the wider determinants of ill health.

This paper considers the differences between how accountability operates in the NHS today, and how it will operate after implementation of the reforms described above. It then considers what issues these reforms might raise for the way that the health service is held to account further into the future. We begin by defining what we mean by accountability, and how variations in the mechanisms of accountability may be defined in practice.

Defining accountability

'Accountability' is an imprecise and contested concept. It has been described as the process of 'being called to account to some authority for one's actions' (Mulgan 2000, p 555). Bovens (2006, p 3) defines accountability as 'a relationship between an actor and a forum, in which the actor has an obligation to explain and to justify his or her conduct, the forum can pose questions and pass judgment, and the actor may face consequences'. Similar definitions have been put forward elsewhere (Day and Klein 1987; Tuohy 2003; Mulgan 2000, 2003). Despite the variability of definitions, there are some common elements, which have formed the basis for the working definition used in this paper.

Accountability typically refers to a relationship involving answerability, an obligation to report, to give an account of, actions and non-actions. This indicates that there is an assumed expectation of the need to **report and explain**, either in person or in writing. A is accountable to B when the former is obliged to inform B about his or her actions and decisions, to justify them, and potentially to be judged on the basis of the account given. Bovens (2006) emphasises the importance of the account being supported by verifiable information that is made public.

Accountability implies that there may be **consequences** (or sanctions) if the 'account-giver' is not able to satisfy the 'account-holder' that he or she has fulfilled the objectives set or made effective use of the resources allocated. Klein and New (1998) distinguish between 'strong' accountability, where there are sanctions if performance or the account of conduct is unsatisfactory, and 'soft' accountability, where an actor is required to justify performance in public (or at least in a transparent process) but no direct sanctions may apply other than perhaps public shaming.

There have been various attempts to delineate **types** of accountability, distinguishing, for example, between political, administrative and market accountability. Political accountability involves the government or its agents having responsibility to be accountable to the public through elections and similar constitutional devices. Administrative accountability relates more to the holding to account of civil servants through hierarchical reporting arrangements and by external regulatory bodies and commissions.

We have taken a pragmatic approach to identifying the specific types of accountability relationship that apply for providers and commissioners of NHS care in England.

This typology draws on the literature in this area, but is predominantly informed by our analysis of the actual relationships in place in the current system and those proposed in the future reforms. This typology applies to both the current and future system, but it is the combination of accountability regimes in practice that may differ.

The following types of accountability are used in this paper to differentiate the accountability relationships that are seen for providers and commissioners of NHS care.

- **Scrutiny**: a type of accountability in which the account holder receives a detailed account of performance within a particular area for which the account giver is being held to account. The implication of accountability based on scrutiny is that the account holder is actively searching for problems within the area of performance.

- **Contract**: through contracts, account holders (eg, commissioners) will hold account givers (eg, providers) to account for meeting the agreed objectives as defined by contract.

- **Management**: managerial accountability is defined as answerability to an account holder in accordance with agreed performance criteria. Typically, such accountability focuses on inputs, outputs and outcomes (Day and Klein 1987) or the resources used to achieve these objectives (Sinclair 1995). Managerial accountability differs from regulation in that it may be applied *ex post facto* (ie, responding to performance) as opposed to *ex ante* (ie, defining a minimum standard of performance), and is usually based on a hierarchy of authority and control.

- **Regulation**: as described above, regulation involves the setting of *ex ante* standards, in which the account holder has clearly defined *post hoc* intervention powers or sanctions. The regulatory relationship is not necessarily hierarchical and the regulator is typically independent. The criteria by which actors are held to account within a regulatory relationship are predominantly minimum standards, rather than developmental or focused on quality improvement. Regulation can be seen in the current system through the relationship between providers and the Care Quality Commission, and between foundation trusts and Monitor.

- **Electoral**: electoral accountability is defined as voters holding to account a representative that they have elected to a particular post. The most obvious examples are the relationship between citizens and parliament, and citizens and local government, where individuals vote in elections and then periodically hold these governing bodies to account for their decisions or actions. Traditionally, citizens delegate some of their account-holding role to other bodies throughout the term of government – for instance, elected representatives or the media.

The different forms of accountability and their distribution between the range of actors are believed to have variable impacts. For instance, electoral accountability is assumed to enable responsible and informed actors to make decisions with more knowledge about – and also with more ability to respond to – local needs than distant officials. Alternatively, distribution of accountability to multiple providers and purchasers through contractual accountability – at least some of which are supposed to be competing to a certain extent in a market or quasi-market context – is intended to create a self-managing system and avoid unnecessary bureaucracy.

The next section describes the current and future accountability relationships (and associated mechanisms) for providers and commissioners of NHS-funded care, drawing particular attention to novel aspects of accountability that arise from the coalition government's reforms.

Current and future accountability relationships for commissioners and providers

In this section we describe the formal accountability relationships that commissioners and providers of NHS care are currently subject to, and how these are set to change under the programme of reform. At the time of writing, many of the reforms described here are the subject of heated political debate and have not yet received legislative approval.

Commissioners

Current accountability arrangements for commissioners

Primary care trusts (PCTs) are responsible for 80 per cent of the NHS budget and are the main commissioners of health services under the current system. They are held to account for their performance through the following formal relationships:

- **management** by their local strategic health authority (SHA) and, potentially, the Secretary of State for Health

- **regulation** by the Care Quality Commission (CQC) in relation to the quality of commissioning

- **scrutiny** by the Audit Commission for managing finances and effective use of resources

- **scrutiny** by overview and scrutiny committees located in local authorities and by patient and public representatives in the form of local involvement networks (LINks)

- **scrutiny** by externally appointed non-executive directors (NEDs) who sit on their boards.

PCTs are subject to potentially strong performance management by SHAs and the Secretary of State. SHAs manage PCTs in line with Department of Health policy, including national performance targets and other 'vital sign' indicators, 'world class commissioning' competencies and plans for improving 'quality, innovation, productivity and prevention' in the health service, known as the QIPP challenge.

In legal terms, SHAs have powers to 'give directions to a [PCT] about its exercise of any function' (Her Majesty's Government 2006, section 20). They have the power to 'escalate' problems with PCT performance to the NHS chief executive and, in specific circumstances, may (on behalf of the NHS chief executive) impose temporary appointments on the board or initiate action to suspend or remove board members. The Secretary of State for Health also has general powers to direct PCTs in relation to any of their functions.

Regulation of the quality of commissioning was introduced for the first time in 2008/09 under the Healthcare Commission (the CQC's predecessor). This included assessment of the quality of PCTs' commissioning (in relation to 'core standards, existing commitments and national priorities') and financial management (based on an Audit Commission assessment). The Healthcare Commission had the power to report weak performance to the Secretary of State, but had no other sanction powers.

In 2009, the Healthcare Commission was replaced by the CQC, which initiated a performance review for 2009/10, although, following the formation of the new government, this was reduced in scale to the publication of a limited selection of 'benchmarking data' with no overall scores for performance. It has since been confirmed that this review of commissioning performance will no longer be part of the CQC's remit.

The Audit Commission carries out an annual assessment of how well PCTs manage their finances and deliver value for money based on local auditor evaluations of their accounts. The commission does not itself have any powers of sanction, but does publish its results, and local auditors can refuse to sign off accounts.

In terms of accountability to the local population, PCTs are subject to scrutiny by two types of organisation intended to represent the interests of patients and the public in the local area: overview and scrutiny committees, which sit in upper-tier local authorities such as county, borough and unitary councils, and LINks, which comprise local voluntary sector organisations co-ordinated by a 'host' organisation.

Overview and scrutiny committees are made up of elected local councillors and at least one dedicated scrutiny officer, and are charged with scrutinising the activities of PCTs (as well as NHS provider trusts and foundation trusts) in relation to the 'planning, provision and operation' of health services in their local area. Overview and scrutiny committees have the power to require local NHS officers to appear before them to answer questions, and to require local NHS bodies to provide any information requested. All NHS trusts, including PCTs, have a duty to respond to the reports and recommendations of overview and scrutiny committees if they are requested to do so, and they are 'encouraged to implement recommendations or provide reasons why no action is taken' (Department of Health 2003b).

PCTs are also bound to consult overview and scrutiny committees on 'substantial' variations to, or developments of, services, and overview and scrutiny committees may refer such matters to the Secretary of State where they find that a proper consultation has not taken place or that the decision reached is not in the interests of the 'local health service'. These arrangements suggest a form of indirect electoral accountability. However, research has demonstrated that this line of accountability is normally not regarded as rigorous by NHS organisations (Storey *et al* 2010).

LINks are intended to represent the voices of local service users and the public in relation to health services. They are made up of pre-existing local voluntary organisations and are co-ordinated by a 'host' organisation commissioned by the local authority. PCTs (and NHS provider trusts) are legally bound to allow members of LINks to enter their premises and observe their activities (within certain limits). PCTs are required to respond to reports produced by LINks, which also make annual reports to the Secretary of State on their findings.

In this way, these two local forms of accountability involve scrutiny and the possibility of referring matters for the attention of the Secretary of State, but they do not in themselves involve sanctions.

PCTs are also subject to internal scrutiny by the externally appointed chair and non-executive directors who sit on their boards alongside executive members. These individuals are legally appointed by the Secretary of State, though in practice this is delegated to the NHS Appointments Commission, which also has powers to seek resignation or to terminate appointments. NEDs have a duty to 'ensure the board acts in the best interests of the public and is fully accountable to the public for the services provided by the organisation and the public funds it uses' (Department of Health and NHS Appointments Commission 2004, p 6) and are 'appointed by the NHS Appointments Commission on behalf of the local community' (Department of Health 2003a).

However as Thorlby *et al* (2008) point out, there is 'no role for local communities in the selection of those individuals' (p 25) and the Department of Health has elsewhere specified that 'Non-executive directors do not "represent" the public. They are there to govern the organisation, by using their experiences in other fields and as residents in the areas they serve' (Department of Health 2004).

It is also debatable whether non-executive derectors are sufficiently independent to hold trusts to account in a meaningful way, since they are members of the board and are jointly responsible with executive members for setting objectives for the organisation and for its performance. On the other hand, they are not full-time servants of the organisation and they do have specific responsibilities to challenge and scrutinise the decisions of the other board members. They thus have to maintain a difficult balance, to be 'challenging yet supportive, independent yet involved' and to 'maintain independence yet not be aloof, uninformed or peripheral' (Likierman 2006).

PCTs are also required to hold board meetings in public, though we would define this as a matter of transparency rather than accountability in the strict sense, since they are not required in that context to offer an explanation of their actions to those attending such meetings.

Overall, in practice, top-down management from the SHA has been the principal accountability relationship for PCTs as commissioners.

In 2005, the government introduced a voluntary scheme in which commissioning decisions could be devolved to primary care service providers – GPs, nurses and other primary care professionals. Under the policy, GP practices were given virtual budgets to 'buy' health services for their population, with PCTs continuing to hold the 'real' money. Some PCTs have gone further and formally handed over commissioning responsibilities to practice-based commissioning groups. Under these arrangements, the practice-based commissioning leads become accountable officers and the PCT's professional executive committee acts as a senate in which decisions that apply to all practice-based commissioning groups are made.

Evaluations of practice-based commissioning suggest that the governance and accountability mechanisms are complex and confusing. There are no formal mechanisms available to PCTs for holding GPs to account for their commissioning decisions (Curry *et al* 2008). One issue has been the legal status of practice-based commissioning consortia. In some areas, these developed into legal entities by forming limited partnerships. However, the majority of locality groups and practice consortia were not regarded as formal legal entities. As such, the practice-based commissioning groups had no statutory basis, and were required to operate within the governance framework of PCTs.

Emergent and future accountability arrangements for commissioners

Under the government's reform plans, responsibility for the majority of commissioning will be transferred to 'GP consortia' – self-organised clusters of GP practices led by an accountable officer. GP consortia will have the following formal accountability relationships:

- **management** by a new national NHS Commissioning Board

- **management** by the Secretary of State through 'standing rules'

- **regulation** by Monitor, reconstituted as a new economic regulator

- **scrutiny** by new health and wellbeing boards based in local authorities; by a separate 'scrutiny function' in local authorities; and by local HealthWatch organisations, which are to take over from LINks

- **scrutiny** of consortia's consolidated annual accounts by the National Audit Office.

A new national body, independent of the Department of Health and accountable to the Secretary of State, will be established to provide 'national leadership' on commissioning. Called the NHS Commissioning Board, it will be charged with holding consortia to account for their 'stewardship of NHS resources' and the 'outcomes they achieve as commissioners' (Department of Health 2010a, p 28). An accountable officer within each consortium will be legally responsible for ensuring a consortium:

- complies with its financial duties

- promotes improvement in the quality of services it commissions

- provides value for money.

The NHS Commissioning Board will be charged with authorising consortia on the basis that they are capable of meeting their statutory responsibilities. As part of this process, each consortium will have to submit a proposed constitution, which will be made publicly available, setting out:

- the geographic area for which it is responsible

- the arrangements for discharging its statutory functions, eg, in relation to public and patient engagement

- the governance arrangements, including procedures for decision-making.

There are no specific requirements on how consortia should be governed; unlike their predecessor organisations, they will not be required to have a board with non-executive members, or to hold their board meetings in public.

Together with the National Institute for Health and Clinical Excellence (NICE), the NHS Commissioning Board will develop a 'commissioning outcomes framework' that will be used to measure health outcomes and the quality of care experienced by each consortium's patients.

The framework is to be developed by the NHS Commissioning Board on the basis of the NHS Outcomes Framework (for which the NHS Commissioning Board is accountable to the Secretary of State). The government has proposed that it should include 'information on the quality of health care services commissioned by consortia, including patient-reported outcome measures and patient experience, and their management of NHS resources' (Department of Health

2010c, p 9). The NHS Commissioning Board will make an annual assessment of how effectively the consortia are improving outcomes and meeting their statutory duties, and a 'quality premium' will see a proportion of GP practice income linked to the outcomes practices achieve together as consortia. The NHS Commissioning Board will also produce commissioning guidance that consortia will be obliged to consider when developing their own commissioning plans.

If the NHS Commissioning Board finds that a consortium has failed or is failing to discharge any of its functions, or considers that there is a 'significant risk' that it will do so, the NHS Commissioning Board will be able to:

■ direct the consortium about how to discharge its functions

■ replace its accountable officer

■ vary its constitution

■ dissolve the consortium.

Secondary legislation is set to define the procedures the NHS Commissioning Board will have to follow before it can intervene, and this will determine how easily the NHS Commissioning Board can exercise these powers.

The government has stipulated that, in contrast to the relationships between PCTs, SHAs and the Secretary of State, the NHS Commissioning Board will not have general powers of direction over consortia: '[the NHS Commissioning Board] will be less of a hierarchical performance manager than a quasi-regulator of commissioners, operating on the basis of clear and transparent rules, within well-defined statutory powers' (Department of Health 2010e, p 63). However, in evidence to the House of Commons Health Committee in November 2010, Andrew Lansley, Secretary of State for Health, said the board 'will be responsible for the performance management, through the commissioning framework, of the NHS commissioning consortiums across the country' (House of Commons Health Committee 2010b). Furthermore, the nominated chief executive of the NHS Commissioning Board, David Nicholson, has indicated that he sees the board as having a wider role than solely providing a safety net for isolated cases of failure, writing in a recent letter to the NHS that the NHS Commissioning Board 'will offer a spectrum of support, from empowering and facilitating success, to intervening to support consortia in difficulty' (Nicholson 2011).

The nature of the NHS Commissioning Board's role remains underdetermined, but the potential for it to play a strong performance-management role has prompted us to classify this link between the NHS Commissioning Board and consortia as essentially a managerial relationship.

The NHS Commissioning Board will itself have responsibilities for commissioning primary care services (including primary medical services) and some specialised and complex services. The NHS Commissioning Board is accountable to the Secretary of State for:

- NHS commissioning expenditure

- the financial stability of commissioners

- performance against its annual mandate, issued by the Secretary of State.

This mandate will specify the objectives that the board should be seeking to achieve in the coming year and 'any requirements that the Secretary of State considers it necessary to impose on the Board for the purpose of ensuring that it achieves those objectives' (House of Commons Bill 2010–11, part 1, clause 13A[2]). The NHS Commissioning Board will be bound by legislation to 'seek to achieve' the objectives and 'comply with any arrangements so specified'.

There do not appear to be separate additional accountabilities in relation to the NHS Commissioning Board's own commissioning responsibilities.

The Secretary of State will also have specific powers of intervention in relation to consortia and the NHS Commissioning Board by issuing 'standing rules' that can impose requirements on how these commissioners exercise their functions. Through creating regulations, the Secretary of State will be able to require that commissioning contracts issued by either body contain particular clauses and, more generally, that the board or consortia must arrange for specific services to be provided, in a particular way, within a particular time period, and/or to particular groups of people. The Secretary of State will have an even broader power to create regulations that can require the NHS Commissioning Board and consortia 'to do such other things as the Secretary of State considers necessary for the purposes of the health service' (House of Commons 2010–11, part 1, clause 16). However, regulations created under this provision would have to be approved by both Houses of Parliament.

Monitor, the foundation trust regulator, is to be made 'economic regulator' for the whole health system. This new Monitor will have the power to investigate any practices by individuals or organisations that it suspects might prevent, restrict or distort competition, or be an abuse of a dominant market position. It will have the power to:

- issue directions to organisations to take (or stop) particular actions

- issue fines following an infringement

- apply to a court to disqualify directors of an organisation (in the case that an agreement or practice has prevented, restricted or distorted competition)

- refer a particular market to the Competition Commission for investigation.

The Bill also makes a provision for subsequent regulations to require that, in the case of a serious breach of competition rules, consortia or the NHS Commissioning Board may be required by Monitor to put a service out to tender.

The Audit Commission, which currently publishes assessments of the financial management of commissioners and whether they make effective use of their resources, is set to be abolished by 2012. However consortia will be required to present audited accounts to the NHS Commissioning Board, which will, in turn, present a consolidated version of these accounts, together with the NHS Commissioning Board's own accounts, to the National Audit Office.

Consortia will be subject to scrutiny by three local bodies:

- a scrutiny function within local authorities

- new health and wellbeing boards, also situated in local authorities

- local HealthWatch organisations, which are to take over from LINks.

The scrutiny powers currently conferred directly on to overview and scrutiny committees will instead be granted to the local authority, which can determine how they will be exercised locally. There are also some adjustments to the scrutiny powers themselves. As is currently the case, whoever is exercising the scrutiny function will be able to require officers of NHS commissioners to attend meetings to answer questions and to comply with requests for information. The local authority scrutinisers will also still have a right to refer cases of service change to the Secretary of State, but this will have to be triggered by a meeting of the full council, and can be made only in relation to a limited group of core 'designated' services. These are services for which there is likely to be a 'significant adverse impact' on the health of the population for which the commissioner is responsible if the services are no longer provided (House of Commons 2011, p 98). Local commissioners must apply to the new Monitor to make the case for services to be designated, following local consultation.

A new statutory committee of local authorities, the health and wellbeing boards, will be charged with undertaking local joint strategic needs assessments and developing new joint health and wellbeing strategies. Consortia themselves will have a duty to participate in the boards (although this can be through a 'lead consortia'), and the boards will have the power to scrutinise the commissioning plans of consortia to ensure that they take due account of the joint health and wellbeing strategy. When a consortium submits its plans to the NHS Commissioning Board, it will have to state whether its local health and wellbeing board agrees that it has had due regard to the joint health and wellbeing strategy. The health and wellbeing boards can also 'write formally' to the NHS

Commissioning Board and GP consortia if they think a consortium has not had adequate regard to the strategy. In addition, the health and wellbeing boards will be empowered to require representatives from the NHS Commissioning Board to attend meetings.

Furthermore, consortia will be subject to scrutiny by the successors of LINks, the local HealthWatch organisations (Department of Health 2010d). These will keep the same form and powers as their predecessor organisations, including the power to enter premises and observe the activities of the bodies they scrutinise. Consortia, like PCTs, will be required to respond to reports produced by their local HealthWatch, which will make annual reports to the Secretary of State.

Consortia will be required to make public their constitution (setting out their geographic area, how they will discharge their legal duties and their governance arrangements), their commissioning plans and their remuneration arrangements, and they will be required to hold annual general meetings that are open to the public. This kind of transparency can be said to support other forms of accountability, in particular local scrutiny by local authorities, health and wellbeing boards and local HealthWatch.

In summary, as shown in Tables 1 and 2 below, the government's reform programme promotes a shift from a system that holds commissioners to account through a combination of management, regulation (albeit only briefly) and scrutiny, to one based on regulation and scrutiny alone. However, there is a distinct possibility that the relationship between consortia and the NHS Commissioning Board, and between all commissioners and the Secretary of State, could involve managerial elements (*see* Tables 1 and 2 below).

Table 1 Current accountability relationships for commissioners of NHS care

	SHA	Secretary of State	CQC	OSCs	LINks	Audit Commission	NEDs
PCTs	Managerial	Managerial	Regulatory	Scrutiny	Scrutiny	Scrutiny	Scrutiny

Table 2 Future accountability relationships for commissioners of NHS care

	NHSCB	Health and wellbeing boards	Monitor	Secretary of State	Local authority scrutiny function	Local HealthWatch
GP consortia	Managerial	Scrutiny	Regulatory	Managerial	Scrutiny	Scrutiny
NHSCB	-	Scrutiny	Regulatory	Managerial	-	-

Providers

Current accountability structures for secondary care providers

Currently, secondary care providers of NHS-funded services fall into three main groups:

- NHS trusts

- NHS foundation trusts (which have additional freedoms)

- independent sector providers.

The last of these account for only a relatively small proportion of services, with the majority of NHS-funded care still being provided by NHS trusts and NHS foundation trusts. The previous administration had a policy commitment that all NHS acute and mental health trusts should reach foundation trust status before 2014 (a postponement of previous targets), and by early spring 2011 more than half of acute and mental health trusts had gained such status.

NHS trusts

NHS trusts without foundation status are currently subject to a host of formal accountability mechanisms, comprising:

- **managerial** relationships with PCTs, SHAs and the Secretary of State for Health

- a **regulatory** relationship with the CQC

- **scrutiny** by local authority overview and scrutiny committees and LINks, supported by the publication of quality accounts

- **scrutiny** by the Audit Commission

- **scrutiny** by externally appointed non-executive directors (NEDs) who sit on their boards.

The formal management relationship between PCTs as commissioners and NHS trusts is modelled on a contractual relationship, using nationally established standard contracts (although they are technically agreements in this context and are not legally binding), which include required performance standards. Sanctions for breaches by NHS trusts include issuing exception reports, which are sent to the local SHA and the CQC; withholding payment; and suspending or terminating the 'contract'.

The latest version of the acute contract includes requirements to provide a particular range of essential services: delivering agreed volumes of different activities; meeting clinical and service quality standards; and performance on other nationally established priorities such as meeting the 18-week maximum waiting time target, reducing the number of mixed-sex wards and reducing health care-acquired infections.

Under a national scheme known as Commissioning for Quality Improvement (CQIN), a small proportion of a trust's income (1.5 per cent in 2010/11) is contingent on it meeting a series of quality standards agreed locally with the PCT.

NHS trusts are also in managerial relationships with the Secretary of State for Health and SHAs, both of which have statutory powers to direct NHS trusts in relation to their exercise of any function. In practice, SHAs have been required to hold trusts to account in relation to their operational and financial performance; the quality of the care and service they provide; and their performance against national policy priorities.

NHS trusts are also regulated by the CQC under a system of quality regulation that has undergone a series of changes since it was first introduced in 1999. Under the latest arrangements, in force from 2010, trusts are legally required to be registered with the CQC in order to provide services. Registration requirements cover what are termed essential safety and quality requirements, and include a range of criteria such as proper use and maintenance of equipment; keeping accurate records; having in place an effective complaints system; and respecting patients and involving them in their care.

In contrast with the previous monitoring system, which involved annual assessments of all trusts based on self-assessment with inspection of 20 per cent, registration now involves continuous assessment based on information from service-users, partner bodies and routine data sets (eg, on mortality), with focused inspection of all organisations individually at least once every two years. This latest set of reforms also granted the CQC stronger powers of sanction for breaches of the registration requirements, including issuing fines and placing conditions on, suspending or cancelling registration – thus removing the right to provide services.

Trusts are also accountable to the Audit Commission, which is responsible for overseeing their accounts, the quality of their financial systems and, more broadly, whether they are delivering value for money. It does not itself have any powers of sanction, but does make its findings public and local auditors can refuse to sign off accounts.

NHS trusts are subject to scrutiny by local authority overview and scrutiny committees and LINks. LINks are intended to hold trusts to account in relation to the interests of patients and the local public. These organisations have the same powers in relation to trusts as they do for PCTs (*see* p 11).

Since 2010, all providers of NHS secondary care have been required to produce quality accounts: public reports of their performance on various locally selected quality measures, together with plans for improvement. These are intended to serve as both a quality improvement tool to encourage trust boards to focus on the quality of care provided by their organisation, and as a public accountability mechanism. Although we would argue that they do not constitute an accountability mechanism in their own right, they can be said to support local scrutinisers in holding the service to account. However, commentators have pointed out that since the quality information contained in the reports is not benchmarked, and often not comparable across organisations because each selects its own measures, the potential for meaningful scrutiny of performance is somewhat limited (Foot *et al* 2011).

Like PCTs, NHS trusts are also required to have externally appointed non-executive directors on their boards and to hold their board meetings in public.

NHS foundation trusts
NHS foundation trust status is granted to high-performing trusts, and establishes trusts as not-for-profit public benefit corporations, which enjoy more freedoms in comparison with their non-foundation trust counterparts, including in relation to borrowing capital; selling assets; retaining surpluses; and developing their own incentive and reward packages for their staff.

The formal mechanisms through which foundation trusts are held to account comprise:

- a **contractual** relationship with PCTs

- **regulatory** relationships with Monitor (charged with authorising foundation trusts) and the CQC

- **scrutiny** by their governors, who are in turn **electorally** accountable to foundation trust members

- **scrutiny** by non-executive directors who sit on the board of directors

- **scrutiny** by LINks and local overview and scrutiny committees, supported by the publication of quality accounts.

Unlike NHS trusts, in formal terms foundation trusts are not managerially accountable to any organisation. They have a legal contractual relationship with PCTs, based either on the same standard contract used as the basis for the agreements between non-foundation trusts and PCTs (covering the same requirements and with the same range of sanctions), or a locally agreed contract if it was already in operation in December 2008 to extend beyond March 2009. They have no formal accountability to SHAs or the Secretary of State.

Foundation trusts have their own regulator, Monitor, a non-Department of Health public body responsible for: assessing eligibility for foundation trust status; granting foundation trust status where trusts are found to meet their terms of authorisation; and monitoring compliance with those terms. These cover provisions relating to the trust's governance arrangements, finances, and provision of agreed mandatory services, education and training. Where a foundation trust is found to be in significant breach of the terms of its authorisation, Monitor has the power to require the board to take specific action; to remove some or all of the directors and governors and appoint replacements; to close services; and, subject to consultation, to dissolve the trust. Monitor is accountable directly to parliament rather than to the government.

Foundation trusts must also be registered with the CQC against the same terms as other NHS trusts. The CQC has the same monitoring and sanctioning powers as it does for NHS trusts, although it is required to co-operate with Monitor in carrying out its duties.

Foundation trusts have a distinct governance arrangement that sets them apart from non-foundation trusts in relation to local accountability mechanisms. Every foundation trust must have a board of governors comprising members of staff and the public (and, in some cases, patients) elected by the foundation trust's members, as well as appointed representatives from local stakeholders including the PCT and the local authority. Through the application process, NHS trusts are required to establish their proposals for the minimum size and composition of their membership. People who live in the area, work for the trust, or have been a patient or service-user there can become members of a foundation trust and as such participate in elections for the trust's elected governors or stand for election themselves. Specialist foundation trusts can draw their membership from anyone across England and Wales, but tend to focus their recruitment on the local geographical area.

The chair of the board of governors is also the chair of the board of directors, providing a link between the two. This means that the chair of the governors is represented on the board of directors, but also that the board of directors has a presence among the governors. Whether this leads to a controlling of the governors in the interest of the directors or a stronger voice for the governors in relation to directors depends on how relationships play out locally.

The governors are charged with appointing the chair and the non-executive directors (and, if appropriate, removing them), and with deciding on their remuneration and allowances. They also scrutinise the trust's annual accounts, and the board of directors must have 'due regard' to the views of the board of governors in preparing the trust's forward plan.

Meetings of the board of governors are required to be open to the public, although a foundation trust's constitution can allow members of the public to be excluded for special reasons. The board of governors is required to convene an annual general meeting within a reasonable timescale after the end of the financial year. There is no legal requirement for foundation trusts to hold their board of directors meetings in public; instead, it is at the discretion of individual foundation trusts to decide whether to allow public access to meetings. A significant number of foundation trusts have opted to hold these meetings in private (Storey *et al* 2010), which signals an important restriction to scrutiny.

Like NHS trusts, foundation trusts are subject to scrutiny by LINks; they must allow members of networks to access their premises (within certain boundaries) and respond to the reports they produce. Foundation trusts are also obliged to appear before overview and scrutiny committees and provide them with information, and to publish quality accounts.

Independent sector providers

Independent sector providers of NHS-funded services are subject to fewer mandatory accountability relationships than are their state-owned counterparts, with the main mechanisms comprising:

- a **contractual** relationship with PCTs

- a **regulatory** relationship with the CQC

- **scrutiny** by LINks supported by the publication of quality accounts.

Like most foundation trusts, independent sector providers have a legal contractual relationship with PCTs using the standard contract. They also have no formal relationship with SHAs or the Secretary of State. They are subject to the same quality registration system with the CQC as are NHS trusts and foundation trusts. They must also publish quality accounts and are subject to the same scrutiny by LINks (in relation to their NHS-funded provision only), although this is set out in contracts with PCTs, which are directed by the Secretary of State to include such clauses, and is not required by legislation. Overview and scrutiny committees do not have powers in relation to independent sector providers.

In summary, as shown in Tables 3 and 4 on page 26, NHS trusts, foundation trusts and independent sector providers have a common regulatory relationship with the CQC and are all subject to scrutiny by LINks. While trusts have a managerial relationship with PCTs, SHAs and the Secretary of State, foundation trusts and independent sector providers have instead a contractual relationship with PCTs (albeit one usually based on the same contract model as is the managerial relationship between trusts and PCTs). In addition, foundation trusts have a regulatory relationship with Monitor, which authorises their status as foundation trusts and regulates them against these terms of authorisation. The Audit Commission scrutinises NHS trusts but not foundation trusts (for which Monitor plays this role) or independent sector providers. Both foundation trusts and NHS trusts have additional local accountability requirements to overview and scrutiny committees. Foundation trusts also have accountability to governors and, through them, to members, comprising staff, the public and patients.

Emergent and future accountability relationships for secondary care providers

The government has confirmed its commitment to the existing target that all trusts should be foundation trusts (or have joined pre-existing foundation trusts) by 2014, and the Health and Social Care Bill gives them the power to repeal the NHS trust model. The government also proposes some broadening of the role of governors and members, by giving governors the power to require:

- some or all of a trust's directors to attend a meeting

- that foundation trusts hold an annual general meeting for their members at which they should discuss the trust's annual report and accounts

- that any changes to the trust's constitution are agreed by the governors and directors (rather than Monitor)

- that any proposed changes to the role of governors can be overturned if a significant majority of the trust's members opposes it at the annual general meeting.

As with commissioners, foundation trusts will continue to be subject to scrutiny by the local HealthWatch and the scrutiny function of local authorities. However, foundation trusts will no longer have a special relationship with Monitor as it becomes a new economic regulator for all providers of NHS-funded care. Requirements to publish quality accounts will continue, which may support scrutiny by governors, local authorities and local HealthWatch organisations.

In summary, from 2014, NHS trusts will cease to exist as an organisational form and the accountability structures of foundation trusts will comprise:

- a **contractual** relationship with GP consortia and (for some services) the NHS Commissioning Board

- a **regulatory** relationship with the CQC on quality and safety, and Monitor in terms of compliance with competition law and service continuity

- **scrutiny** by the local HealthWatch organisation and the scrutiny function of local authorities

- **scrutiny** by governors, some of whom are elected by members, comprising staff and the local public.

The accountability of independent sector organisations will include two new relationships: economic regulation by new Monitor and scrutiny by local authorities, the scrutiny powers of which are to extend to all providers of NHS-funded services. Formal accountability relationships for these providers will comprise:

- a **contractual** relationship with GP consortia and the NHS Commissioning Board

- **regulatory** relationships with the CQC and Monitor

- **scrutiny** by the local HealthWatch and the scrutiny function of local authorities.

The government has expressed enthusiasm for the role of voluntary sector providers in public service provision as part of the Big Society agenda. More specifically, it plans to extend the current 'right to request' programme for community services to the acute sector, giving existing NHS trust staff the right to request that they provide services as social enterprises and to encourage foundation trusts to allow their staff to do the same. This means that the third sector may play a more significant role in the provision of secondary care in the future.

The accountability structures and processes for these organisations will vary to some extent by type. For example, charities with turnovers greater than £5,000 a year must be registered with the regulator, the Charity Commission, which acts to ensure that they comply with the legal requirements relating to their charitable status, works to encourage 'effectiveness and impact', and promotes the public interest in the work of charities. Like their private sector counterparts, third sector organisations will also have a range of internal governance arrangements, some of which – for example, those that are employee-owned or with explicit employee engagement models – will involve stronger internal accountability mechanisms than others.

However, if these new providers win contracts for NHS-funded care, or satisfy requirements such that NHS-funded patients can choose their service, they will be subject to the same accountability requirements as their independent sector counterparts. In these cases, third sector providers will enter into contractual relationships with commissioners, regulatory relationships with the CQC and Monitor (and, in some cases, also with the Charity Commission), and scrutiny by local authorities supported by a requirement that they publish quality accounts.

Thus, the accountability of all secondary care providers will be very similar under the new system, except that independent sector and third sector providers will not be legally required to have governance relationships involving representatives of patients, the public and/or staff.

The changes will result in a shift away from performance management towards a reliance on regulation and contracts, supplemented by local public accountability mechanisms. As the consultation paper on regulating health care providers put it, the government's approach is 'that where specific control mechanisms are needed for providers, these should in general take effect through regulatory licensing and clinically-led contracting, rather than hierarchical management' (Department of Health 2010f, p 3).

Table 3 Current accountability relationships for providers of NHS hospital care

	PCT	SHA	Secretary of State	CQC	Monitor	Audit Comm-ission	LINks	OSCs	Patients/ public	Staff	NEDs
NHS trust	Managerial	Managerial	Managerial	Regulatory	–	Scrutiny	Scrutiny	Scrutiny	–	–	Scrutiny
Foundation trust	Contractual	–	–	Regulatory	Regulatory	–	Scrutiny	–	Scrutiny	Scrutiny	Scrutiny
Independent sector	Contractual	–	–	Regulatory	–	–	Scrutiny	–	Depending on model	Depending on model	–

Table 4 Future accountability relationships for providers of NHS hospital care

	GP consortia	NHSCB	CQC	Monitor	Local HealthWatch	Local authority scrutiny function	Patients/ public	Staff	NEDs
Foundation trust	Contractual	Contractual	Regulatory	Regulatory	Scrutiny	Scrutiny	Scrutiny	–	Scrutiny
Independent sector	Contractual	Contractual	Regulatory	Regulatory	Scrutiny	Scrutiny	Depending on model	Depending on model	Depending on model
Third sector (eg, voluntary sector, social enterprise)	Contractual	Contractual	Regulatory	Regulatory	Scrutiny	Scrutiny	Depending on model	Depending on model	Depending on model

Current accountability arrangements for primary care providers

NHS primary care services are provided by GPs, dentists, community pharmacists and opticians, most of whom are independent contractors. GP practices are currently subject to significantly fewer accountability mechanisms than are secondary care providers. Their accountability relationships comprise:

- a **contractual** relationship with PCTs

- **scrutiny** by LINks.

Most GP practices are in a contractual relationship with their local PCT, based on either a General Medical Services (GMS) or a personal medical services (PMS) contract.

GMS contracts are negotiated nationally, whereas the content of PMS contracts is agreed locally. GMS contracts cover a range of requirements, including:

- access to essential services

- the state of premises

- clinical governance

- providing nationally defined, locally agreed additional services (such as cervical screening and maternity services)

- the number of registered patients that will constitute the practice being full and closed to new patients

- complaints procedures

- systems for staff training and appraisal

- 'having regard' to guidance issued by PCTs and SHAs.

If these requirements are breached, the PCT can:

- terminate the contract

- require the practice to stop undertaking any other business that is considered to be detrimental to its performance under the contract

- issue contract sanctions.

GP practices are subject to scrutiny by LINks and, by 2009, more than one-fifth of practices had voluntarily established their own patient participation groups. These groups seem to be heterogeneous in purpose, form and power; most advise their practice on 'the patient perspective', although relatively few conduct research on the views of the wider practice population. It is not clear whether any of these groups hold any formal powers in relation to their respective practices or routinely scrutinise their activity, but it is worth noting that some practice-based commissioning groups have required their member practices to have a patient participation group.

Community-based providers of NHS-funded dentistry, pharmacy and ophthalmic care are predominantly independent contractors that hold nationally negotiated contracts with their local PCT. These providers are also subject to scrutiny by LINks in the same way as other providers of primary and secondary NHS care.

Emergent and future accountability relationships for primary care providers

The reform programme will see GP practices subject to a greater number of accountability relationships than they are at present, comprising:

- a **contractual** relationship with the NHS Commissioning Board

- **regulation** by the CQC and Monitor

- potentially a **managerial** relationship with GP commissioning consortia

- **scrutiny** by local HealthWatch and the reformed local authority scrutiny function, supported by a new requirement to publish quality accounts.

GP practices will have a contract with the NHS Commissioning Board. The content of these new contracts – performance requirements and associated sanctions – can be determined by the Secretary of State, or delegated to the NHS Commissioning Board to negotiate. The NHS Commissioning Board can, in turn, choose to delegate some of these functions to GP commissioning consortia.

GP practices will also have some kind of formal accountability relationship with the consortium to which they belong. The consortium will be responsible for:

- holding their member practices to account for their stewardship of resources

- driving up the quality of primary medical care

- carrying out primary medical service contract management work on behalf of the NHS Commissioning Board.

The precise nature of this relationship between consortia and GP practices is for local agreement, although there seems to be the potential for this to be a managerial relationship.

The other entirely new accountability relationship for GP practices will be with the regulators: from April 2012, GP practices will be required to be licensed with the CQC (a change put in train by the previous administration) and with new Monitor.

Scrutiny by LINks becomes scrutiny by local HealthWatch, and the scrutiny powers currently held by overview and scrutiny committees, which are to be conferred on local authorities, will now also cover GPs, who will be required to present an officer to answer questions and to provide information on request. Primary care providers will, from 2011/12, also have to produce quality accounts.

Overall, the reforms mean GP practices will be in a greater number of accountability relationships with a host of new players (*see* Tables 5 and 6 opposite). They shift from being subject to scrutiny by LINks, and in a contractual relationship with PCTs, to being subject to regulation by both Monitor and the CQC, scrutiny by the newly expanded scrutiny powers of local authorities and the local HealthWatch, and being accountable to GP consortia in a way that is to be determined locally, but looks likely to involve managerial forms of performance management.

Other providers of NHS-funded primary care – community pharmacists, opticians and dentists – will, as a result of the reforms, contract directly with the NHS Commissioning Board in future. All primary care dentists providing NHS-funded care will also be subject to CQC registration (again, this was already in process under the last government). Primary pharmacy and primary ophthalmic services are currently excluded from registration. It is not yet clear whether any or all of these providers will be subject to licensing with Monitor.

Table 5 Current accountability relationships for general practices

	PCT	LINks
GP practices	Contractual	Scrutiny

Table 6 Future accountability relationships for general practices

	GP consortia	NHSCB	CQC	Monitor	Local HealthWatch	Local authority scrutiny function
GP practices	Managerial?	Contractual	Regulatory	Regulatory	Scrutiny	Scrutiny

Community care providers

The term community health services covers a range of services aimed at preventing illness, managing the effects of long-term conditions, and assisting recovery in patients' homes or community settings. These services include those provided by community nurses and health visitors, speech and language therapists, physiotherapists and school nurses, as well as other health promotion activities and, in collaboration with other providers, maternity services, mental health services and sexual health services.

The majority of these NHS-funded services are currently provided by PCTs' provider arms or their successors (*see* below), although some are also provided by the independent sector, the voluntary sector and NHS trusts. Under the policies of the previous government, from April 2009 all PCT provider arms were required to enter into formal legal contractual relationships with the commissioning arm of the PCT, and thereafter to develop plans to separate their organisations entirely from the PCT, becoming independent social enterprises or foundation trusts, or merging with other NHS provider organisations such as acute trusts.

At the time of writing, plans for PCT provider arms are, in many cases, still in development. Many have requested the right to establish themselves as a social enterprise since this option was established in 2008, and some have already become NHS community trusts *en route* to foundation trust status (Hansard 2010a, 2010b).

Their key accountability relationships are:

- **contractual** relationships with the PCT

- **regulation** by the CQC for some services

- **scrutiny** by LINks

- **management** by SHAs (for PCT-owned providers only).

Future accountability relationships in community services

The new government has committed itself firmly to an any willing provider model in community care services, consolidating the previous government's efforts to require PCT provider arms to separate themselves from PCTs as commissioners, and pushing more strongly for a true market in these services. The operating framework for the NHS in England 2011/12 stated: '... by 1 April 2011 all PCT directly provided community services must have been separated from PCT commissioning functions and the divestment of these services from PCTs completed or substantial progress made towards divestment. There should be a level playing field for all providers' (Department of Health 2010h, paragraphs 2.28 and 2.29, p 19).

Thus, if the government's reforms are implemented, providers of NHS-funded community services will comprise:

- NHS foundation trusts (either community service-specific or as part of acute or mental health foundation trusts)

- third sector (including social enterprise) providers

- independent sector providers.

Their principal accountability relationships will comprise:

- **contractual** relationships with both GP consortia and the NHS Commissioning Board

- **regulation** by the CQC and potentially a regulatory relationship with Monitor

- **scrutiny** by local HealthWatch and by the scrutiny function of local authorities, supported by a new requirement to produce quality accounts.

Will the new accountability system meet the government's policy aims?

The government's reform programme includes a series of stated objectives relevant to the future of accountability in the NHS:

- reducing performance management and central control

- enhancing local accountability

- creating a 'level playing field' on which providers can compete

- increasing transparency through the publication of performance information.

In this section, we examine whether the reforms are likely to achieve these aims.

Is this the end of performance management and central control?

The previous Labour administration's NHS reform policies comprised two major phases: a push to improve performance through the use of targets and strong performance management, followed by policies intended to create a 'self-improving' system organised around market principles and supported by quality regulation. In practice these two approaches came to co-exist, and, despite calls for the service to look out to patients and not up to Whitehall, the accountability regime for the NHS until 2010 continued to be characterised by strong, centralised performance management in addition to contractual mechanisms and a system of quality regulation.

The coalition government made an early commitment to throw out the 'overwhelming importance attached to certain top-down targets' (Department of Health 2010a, paragraph 3.2, p 21) and stated that performance should be driven by patient choice and commissioning, in other words, by market forces and not performance management. In its vision: 'The Secretary of State will hold the NHS to account for improving health care outcomes. The NHS, not politicians, will be responsible for determining how best to deliver this within a clear and coherent national policy framework' (Department of Health 2010a, paragraph 3.4, p 21). So will the new system really mean an end to performance management and centralised control?

The government's reforms will see the dismantling of key parts of the apparatus of the current system of performance management:

- the Secretary of State will no longer have general powers of direction over commissioners

- strategic health authorities (SHAs), which currently act as the main conduit for communication and enforcement of instructions from the Department of Health to primary care trusts (PCTs) and NHS trusts, are to be scrapped

- The NHS trust model, under which hospitals have been subject to general powers of direction from both SHAs and the Secretary of State, will cease to exist.

However, the Health and Social Care Bill (House of Commons 2010–11) also creates the possibility for a strong line of performance management to run down from the Secretary of State to the NHS Commissioning Board and general practice consortia; from the NHS Commissioning Board to GP consortia; and from consortia to GP practices.

To take the Secretary of State's powers first, although he or she will no longer have any general powers of direction (except in cases of emergency), he or she will be empowered to make so-called standing rules, which will impose requirements on consortia and the NHS Commissioning Board as to how they should exercise their functions. These could easily be used to create the kind of performance targets imposed by the previous government. A further opportunity for the Secretary of State to place strong requirements on the NHS Commissioning Board is introduced through the board's mandate.

However, the Health and Social Care Bill also places a requirement on the Secretary of State to act with a view to promoting autonomy in the health service by providing freedom to bodies such as consortia to carry out their duties in the way that they consider most appropriate, and by not imposing unnecessary burdens on such organisations (House of Commons 2010–11, part 1, clause 4).

What sufficient freedom or unnecessary burdens might look like is open to interpretation. It is not clear that this provision would prevent a Secretary of State from using standing rules to create a strong and quite specific set of performance requirements for commissioners that relate to processes as well as outcomes. The current Secretary of State's own political commitments may mean that he does not use these powers in that way, but the point remains that the powers are there should he change his mind, or should he be succeeded by someone with a different approach.

The relationship between the NHS Commissioning Board and GP consortia is less specified in the primary legislation and depends, in part, on the nature of the regulations surrounding the NHS Commissioning Board's right to intervene in cases of failure and on how the NHS Commissioning Board decides to interpret its responsibility for conducting annual performance assessments of consortia. These assessments present an opportunity for the development of a strong management relationship between the NHS Commissioning Board and consortia, reinforced by the NHS Commissioning Board's power to award discretionary payments to consortia. Much will depend on whether the NHS Commissioning Board decides to perform that function in a light-touch or strong-armed way.

The relationship between GP practices and GP consortia has been left to local determination, but the government expects consortia to 'play a key role in working with individual GP practices to drive up the quality of primary medical care' (Department of Health 2010c, paragraph 3.18, p 16), and has said that the consortia may be asked by the NHS Commissioning Board to carry out some contract management work on the NHS Commissioning Board's behalf. Consortia will also have the power to determine how performance-related payments awarded by the NHS Commissioning Board will be distributed among practices. As with the other links in the chain described above, a great deal rests on how actors decide to interpret their powers and how the organisations they are holding to account respond (an issue we return to below).

In contrast, changes for non-foundation trust providers of secondary care services will signal a significant reduction in performance management. Having been subject to the general managerial powers of the Secretary of State and SHAs, NHS providers will, in future, be accountable principally through contract management to their commissioners and subject to the regulatory powers of the Care Quality Commission (CQC) and new Monitor.

In summary, there is undoubtedly less centralised control under the reformed system: the Secretary of State does not have powers of general direction over commissioners and providers, and neither does the NHS Commissioning Board. However, the Secretary of State retains strong and potentially broad powers in relation to the NHS Commissioning Board and commissioning consortia. Although the system is supposed to be characterised by localism, devolution and autonomy, on the commissioning side the chain of command from the centre appears to remain strong.

Will the health service be more locally accountable?

The government's localism agenda includes a broad commitment to strengthening the accountability of government and public services to local people, and in health the government has specifically promised greater 'local democratic legitimacy' for services. So will the government's reform programme make the health service more accountable to the local populations it serves? The reforms modify a number of existing local accountability mechanisms, namely foundation trust governance arrangements and local authority scrutiny powers, as well as introducing health and wellbeing boards. How effective are these mechanisms likely to be?

In future, the transfer of all NHS trusts to foundation trust status, together with some former PCT provider services moving to foundation status, will extend these local accountability arrangements to more NHS organisations. As described in the previous section, the role of governors and members is also set to be broadened, and the current relationship with Monitor will change from one of regulation combined with elements of managerial accountability (Exworthy *et al* 2009) to solely market regulation. Will these local accountability mechanisms provide sufficiently robust oversight?

Evaluations of the impact of the current model of governors and members on the running of foundation trusts have found mixed results. Several studies from the early implementation of the foundation trust model (Day and Klein 2005; Healthcare Commission 2005; Lewis 2005; Lewis and Hinton 2008) describe the challenges trusts faced in developing the new governance structure, with only small numbers of people volunteering for membership, membership being largely unrepresentative of the relevant population, and low turnouts in elections for governors. These studies also noted concerns among governors in terms of the clarity of their role and responsibilities.

More recently, Ham and Hunt concluded that 'governance arrangements in foundation trusts are now established and are becoming increasingly effective' (Ham and Hunt 2008, p 38). For example, they noted that there is greater clarity in the role of the board of governors, that an increasing number of governors participate in a meaningful way in the operation of foundation trusts, and that their presence had made directors and staff more aware of the views of patients and the public.

However, in their joint report on the effectiveness of the then government's NHS reform programme as a whole, the Audit Commission and Healthcare Commission found continued confusion around the role of foundation trust governors and no significant evidence that they had had an impact on the development of trusts (Audit Commission/Healthcare Commission 2008). Governors interviewed for another study (Storey *et al* 2010) reported that they were easily controlled by the chief executive and the boards of directors, and that their input into the strategic operation of foundation trusts was largely passive – as information receivers, rather than actively shaping the organisation.

Taken together, these studies indicate that it might take some years for local governance mechanisms to become effective and, given the mixed findings of more recent studies, that even among more established foundation trusts there could be considerable variation between trusts in the effectiveness of these arrangements.

The existing legal power of governors seems to give them the potential to hold a significant influence over trusts, particularly powers to appoint and remove the chair and non-executive directors, but the extent to which this translates into a powerful 'holding to account' in practice depends on how these relationships play out locally.

However, the governance arrangements of foundation trusts hold out greater promise of enhancing local accountability than do those of GP commissioning consortia. As we noted in our description of changes to commissioning, unlike their predecessor organisations, consortia are not required to have boards with non-executive directors or to hold their meetings in public. It is currently unclear how or to what extent they will be locally accountable.

Two other significant changes to local accountability structures are the increased role for local authorities in relation to health through changes to local authorities' overview and scrutiny powers, and the establishment of health and wellbeing boards, the responsibilities of which will include scrutinising NHS commissioning plans (in addition to leadership in public health, which is not covered here).

Local authorities' overview and scrutiny committees have been empowered to scrutinise planning and provision of the health service since 2003, with powers to require NHS officers to appear before them and to provide information, and to refer matters to the Secretary of State. PCTs and NHS trusts have also been required to consult these committees on any 'substantial' changes to health services. The government's plans place some limits on these powers by requiring that local authorities be consulted about substantial changes to only a limited range of 'designated' services, and requiring a full council meeting to trigger a referral to the Secretary of State. However, they also extend the power of local authorities to require representations from NHS officers and information from NHS bodies to all providers of NHS-funded services.

The most extensive review to date of the effectiveness of existing health overview and scrutiny found that the committees had developed constructive relationships with local NHS organisations and individuals that could help them to provide 'collaborative challenge', but that strains on resources for support and the demands of contributing to national government consultations and reviews by the regulator placed limits on their abilities to conduct their own reviews of services (Coleman et al 2009). In future, scrutiny powers will be conferred on local authorities and not directly to overview and scrutiny committees, so it will be up to local authorities to decide how this function is to be organised and conducted.

Given current and future pressures on the resources of local authorities, there is a real risk that, at best, this scrutiny function will not enjoy the increase in resources that research suggests it needs in order to be effective, and more probably that resourcing will be further reduced. This could significantly inhibit the effectiveness of this accountability function.

The establishment of health and wellbeing boards and their proposed relationship with consortia creates a new form of accountability for local commissioners to local authorities. However, the power of the health and wellbeing boards amounts principally to commissioners being required to 'have regard to' their joint health and wellbeing strategies in the formulation of their commissioning plans, which is arguably comparable to existing requirements for NHS bodies to have regard to local area agreements (which are set to be abolished). Although requiring participation in the health and wellbeing boards may help promote joint working at a local level, it is not clear whether these boards will be sufficiently empowered to hold consortia to account, particularly in the context of the relationship between consortia and the NHS Commissioning Board, which may involve a strong form of quasi-regulation and/or performance management. Furthermore, if health and wellbeing boards lack (or are perceived to lack) any real influence, they may face significant difficulties in attracting a sufficiently experienced and authoritative membership.

Finally, Local Involvement Networks (LINks) are set to be rebranded as local HealthWatch organisations. Much of the form and activities of local HealthWatch groups will remain the same as for their predecessor organisation. It is difficult to measure how effective these organisations are as account holders. One possible proxy for this is whether their scrutiny of organisations prompts the organisation to make changes to the way it provides services.

The latest annual review, based on data returns from LINks organisations, found that the networks had produced an estimated 1,300 reports and sets of recommendations in 2009/10, but that only around one-third of these had (in the opinion of the LINks) led to a service review or change (Department of Health 2010g). The data show considerable geographic variation: although 54 per cent of LINks said that they had had failed to stimulate any service change through their PCTs, 11 per cent said they had prompted three or four changes, and a further 11 per cent reported prompting five or more service changes in their area.

These figures suggest that this form of voice can be effective in holding the service to account, but that such examples may make up only a minority of cases, indicating that these arrangements cannot be relied upon to deliver effective local accountability consistently. However, it should be noted that these figures had improved on the previous year, suggesting that these organisations may grow in strength as they bed down, and that the government's decision to continue with these existing structures presents an opportunity for them to build on the progress already made, rather than for replacement organisations to spend the next few years seeking to establish themselves. The establishment of a national HealthWatch organisation, situated in the CQC and with its chair having a place on the CQC's board, should give local HealthWatch a more powerful voice at a national level, which may raise its profile and strengthen its membership locally, though we are doubtful whether national HealthWatch would carry much power in relation to Monitor, for example.

Overall, although the reforms mean a greater reliance on local mechanisms for holding providers and commissioners to account, we are pessimistic about whether the changes will strengthen the accountability of the NHS at a local level.

Do the reforms create a more level playing field for providers?

In the current system, providers of secondary care are subject to quite different types of accountability relationships depending on their ownership status. Under the government's commitment to a market for care provision, in which 'all providers of NHS care should be able to compete on a level playing field' (Department of Health 2010f, p 3), these providers ought to be subject to equally (and ideally minimally) onerous requirements to account for their activities.

Recent studies of the extent to which there is a level playing field for providers of NHS care have identified many disparities in the conditions for state and non-state providers, such as:

- favourable pension arrangements for the NHS as an employer

- differences in requirements to provide education and training

- cheaper access to capital for the NHS

- cultural behaviours within the service that favour NHS providers

- NHS providers having to cross-subsidise the large overheads associated with accepting emergency admissions (Brereton and Gubb 2010; House of Commons 2010–11).

There has been no work dealing specifically with the impact of the different requirements placed on NHS and non-NHS providers in terms of accounting for their performance and being subject to the policies and directions of central government and SHAs. Under the current system, NHS trusts are subject to twice as many formal accountability mechanisms as independent sector providers of NHS-funded care (*see* Table 3, page 26), which could be considered a competitive disadvantage. The reforms will mean that the accountability requirements on independent sector and public sector providers of secondary care will be harmonised and almost identical. The one significant difference will be in requirements relating to their internal governance arrangements. For foundation trust governors, elected by staff and the local public and appointed to represent local stakeholders, will have increased powers in relation to the board. An independent sector provider may be also be overseen by a board, but its composition and accountabilities will vary depending on its organisational form. Nonetheless, the reforms represent a significant reduction in the variation in relationships and mechanisms by which these providers are held to account, creating a more level playing field for secondary care providers.

In terms of primary care, all providers of general medical services are likely to face the same set of accountability relationships with external organisations regardless of their ownership status. GP practices are in competition with secondary care providers only at the margins of their activities, so the theory of a level playing field in relation to equalising the burden of accountability requirements for the sake of fair competition between primary and secondary care is less relevant. However, general medical service providers may find themselves subject to more accountability requirements than their secondary care colleagues in the future, having accountability to the CQC, Monitor, local authorities and local HealthWatch organisations, and, in addition, having a new, potentially strong managerial, accountability relationship with their consortia and the NHS Commissioning Board.

Will publishing performance information make the service more accountable?

The coalition government has emphasised its commitment to making data on performance across government and the public services publicly available wherever possible as part of its drive to open up government to scrutiny by the public. This is a form of 'giving an account', which does not include requirements to provide an explanation of performance or intrinsic sanctions for any poor performance described by such accounts. Because of this, information and transparency of themselves fall outside of our definition of accountability.

However, such information becomes potentially more powerful when it is combined with other accountability mechanisms, such as local scrutiny arrangements, or an individual patient's right to exercise a choice about the provider of secondary care. If transparency is to be enhanced, and to support actors in holding organisations to account, information needs to be robust, comprehensible and relevant to scrutinisers, the public and patients. One of the main current vehicles for making performance information available to the public – quality accounts – does not yet meet these demands. The government has confirmed that it plans to continue with the existing requirement that providers of NHS-funded acute, mental health, learning disability and ambulance services must produce annual quality accounts, and that this requirement will be extended to community and primary care providers over the next two years. However, as Foot *et al* (2011) have pointed out, because quality accounts also serve as quality improvement tools for local boards, boards have been given local discretion on which indicators of quality they focus on in the accounts, which means there are no guaranteed points of comparison or external 'benchmarks' against which interested parties can interpret performance data. They recommended that quality accounts should, in future, be required to include some national, standardised indicators.

There are also challenges associated with non-expert scrutinisers, patients and members of the public interpreting data on clinical performance. Research from the United States found that patients and carers make little use of published performance data because they have trouble understanding the content – for example, whether 'high' or 'low' on particular measures is a good or a bad thing (Hibbard and Jewett 1997). More recent research conducted in England by The King's Fund has highlighted the high levels of numeracy required in order to understand and compare clinical quality data, concluding that patients need more support in order to make this data meaningful (Boyce *et al* 2010).

There are also major challenges associated with communicating the uncertainty and expert disagreement around what can be deduced from individual clinical indicators such as hospital mortality ratios. The government is committed to stimulating an innovative private market in information processing and packaging, which it would argue will make information more accessible and meaningful for patients. The challenges of developing and analysing robust clinical performance data means there ought to be a system for accrediting information providers and quality assuring published information (The King's Fund 2011a).

If these challenges were overcome, and scrutinisers, patients and the public could easily access robust, meaningful and comprehensible information on the performance of health care organisations, what action could they take if they found that performance to be wanting?

Local HealthWatch will provide one of the main mechanisms for local accountability through scrutiny.

Another mechanism is patient choice. If a provider is revealed to be performing poorly or in undesirable ways, individual patients can employ the sanction of choosing not to be treated by that provider for non-urgent care at the point of GP referral. This would deny the provider that patient's 'custom' and, so the theory goes, send a signal to the provider that it needs to improve its service.

However, patients have had this right to choose for five years, and yet a major government-funded evaluation of its implementation confirmed government statistics that show that only around half of the patients eligible recall having been offered a choice, and that two-thirds of those who were offered a choice opted for their local hospital (Dixon *et al* 2010b). Very few patients (4 per cent) who recalled having been given a choice had consulted the NHS Choices website, and only 6 per cent had consulted patient leaflets – both of which sources provide comparable performance information on hospitals. The same study found that hospitals perceive GP referral patterns to have a much greater impact on their intake than do the choices of patients.

Furthermore, it is not clear that patient choice constitutes an accountability mechanism *per se*: although it might prompt an organisation to be sensitive to the views of its patients, it does not, in itself, require organisations to report and explain their behaviour.

In summary, although greater transparency of information may be a valuable thing in its own right, experience to date suggests that this will not necessarily have a significant impact on the accountability of services to their local populations. Such information might be put to good use by local HealthWatch organisations, although evidence suggests that their effectiveness is likely to vary.

Will the system be fit for purpose?

There are many questions we might want to ask of an accountability regime beyond whether it fulfils the political aspirations set for it. Here we suggest three:

- Is the system coherent – does it avoid overlaps or gaps?
- Does it target the right actors – who is being held to account?
- What will accountability relationships be like in practice?

Is the system coherent?

One major potential overlap in the system is for GP commissioning consortia. The new system could create competing, potentially conflicting, demands on GP consortia as a result of their dual accountability to the NHS Commissioning Board on the one hand, and local health and wellbeing boards on the other.

In its December 2010 command paper (Department of Health 2010e), the government stated categorically that consortia are accountable first to the NHS Commissioning Board, but acknowledged that further work was required in order to manage the potential for consortia to be under conflicting requirements as a result of their being also accountable to the health and wellbeing boards. As described earlier (pp 10–31), the Health and Social Care Bill (House of Commons 2010–11) places various requirements on consortia to have regard to the health and wellbeing boards' health and wellbeing strategies, and empowers health and wellbeing boards to 'write formally' to the NHS Commissioning Board where a consortium fails to do so.

In an effort to bring together the two sets of accountability requirements being imposed on consortia by the NHS Commissioning Board and health and wellbeing boards, the Bill also requires that the NHS Commissioning Board must appoint a representative to join the health and wellbeing boards to assist in the preparation of the joint strategic needs assessment or health and wellbeing strategy, and requires health and wellbeing boards to have regard to the NHS Commissioning Board's mandate when developing their strategy.

Will this be enough to ensure that consortia do not find themselves subject to conflicting demands? Although these various mechanisms may be able to serve a useful communication role, requiring organisations to have only 'due regard' to a particular piece of guidance in developing their own plans is a fairly weak legal constraint. However, in practice, given the potential strength of the NHS Commissioning Board, consortia are likely to focus predominantly on their performance against the NHS Commissioning Framework rather than on whether they are commissioning in line with local plans drawn up by the health and wellbeing boards.

Does it target the right actors?

Under the current arrangements, accountability is focused on holding to account either an organisation, such as an NHS trust or primary care trust (PCT), or an individual (through professional regulation, not discussed in this paper). However, given that patients' experience of care will, in future, often span a number of organisations, and may be significantly affected by the nature and quality of the links between those organisations, there is a case for holding the service to account for the whole of that collaborative care process, rather than solely its component parts. Fragmentation of care across a number of organisations risks lack of continuity of care for patients, who may find it difficult to hold anyone to account for this crucial aspect of their experience.

The government's vision that the NHS Commissioning Board should hold consortia to account for the outcomes achieved by the care they commission may create the opportunity for commissioning for outcomes along particular service lines or for defined patient groups, rather than commissioning institutions for volumes of care. The NHS Commissioning Board will be able to specify the structure of the tariff in future, and the Bill suggests that this could cover one or more services, depending on the specific clinical area or intervention. This would require new ways of holding partnerships, networks or chains of organisations to account. The NHS Commissioning Board will also be able to develop standard contracts, which could, for example, introduce contract terms that require organisations to collaborate to improve outcomes.

This would be a new and more radical way of working, and would depend on these requirements placing a strong 'pull' on organisations to counterbalance the systems of quality and economic regulation that focus on individual organisations.

Although the Care Quality Commission (CQC) is technically focused on activities, in practice the organisation delivering the regulated activity is the one that must register with the quality regulator. The licensing system for Monitor also appears to be intended to hold organisations to account. Previous attempts to hold cancer networks to account for achieving particular process targets involved no tangible sanctions and 'soft' forms of governance in which collaboration across organisations and professional groups was emphasised, with network boards established to oversee strategic decision-making on behalf of the networks. However, in practice, partnership working and sharing knowledge across organisational and professional boundaries were superseded by top-down control through performance management – organisations were predominantly focused on meeting the targets and standards as set for their individual institution (Addicott 2005).

Commissioners need to be supported to focus commissioning on outcomes for patients. This will require new types of accountability relationship to be established, in which lead providers take responsibility for performance and share the risks and rewards of contracts with their collaborators, or commissioners contract with networks or integrated providers. Current US health policy is experimenting with holding collaborations to account for the quality and cost of care through Accountable Care Organisations (*see* Fisher and Shortell 2010). Evaluations of these experiments are still at an early stage, but we should be sure to draw lessons from their experiences to support the development of best practice in England.

What will accountability relationships be like in practice?

The structures of accountability described in this report set out the formal powers and responsibilities of organisations in the system and provide an important framework within which they interact. However, much of the reality of an accountability regime is determined by how relationships play out in practice, by the pre-existing culture and behaviour of organisations, and by perceptions of the authority or power of actors. As an example, although foundation trusts are not formally accountable to strategic health authorities (SHAs) or the Department of Health, research suggests that, in practice, the Department of Health and some SHAs have continued to seek to hold foundation trusts to account, and that the latter have responded accordingly (Exworthy *et al* 2009; Dixon *et al* 2010a). Leaked correspondence between the chairman of Monitor and the NHS chief executive showed Monitor criticising the Department of Health for issuing letters to foundation trusts that were 'instructive' and 'directive' in nature, claiming that such letters were compromising the intended independence of foundation trusts (Carvel 2008).

How relationships play out in the new system will depend on the cultural baggage players bring with them, and on the personalities at the top of key organisations such as the NHS Commissioning Board, Monitor and the CQC, as well as the Secretary of State. The abolition of SHAs and PCTs and the restructuring of the Department of Health might mitigate the risk of some patterns of interaction being repeated, but individual actors may bring old habits with them, which could have a strong influence on how such bodies co-operate.

However, unlike their counterparts in PCTs from whom they are taking over the mantle of commissioning, GPs are not schooled in NHS management and have operated as independent contractors to the NHS, in a culture that is entrepreneurial and largely free from statutory obligations or reporting requirements. There is a chance that GPs will not be in the thrall of central institutions such as the NHS Commissioning Board as much as their predecessors were, which may act as a counterbalance to the strong performance management powers present in the system.

Analysis of previous reforms indicates that new forms of accountability are likely to be superimposed over the old forms rather than replacing them entirely. Both Hood *et al* (2000, p 302) and Addicott (2005) identified such layering in regulation and accountability relationships. Hood argued that the previous government promoted deregulation of public services, while at the same time increasing the number of arms-length regulatory bodies. More than a decade ago he suggested that it seemed likely that a pattern in which regulators 'neither fully compete nor fully collaborate [and] follow no general or consistent principles' was likely to continue (p 302). Addicott reinforces this conclusion, arguing that these overlapping and conflicting regimes generate confusion and frustration, with tensions continuing over a long period of time as there is no return to a single coherent process. It is possible that emergent accountability processes and relationships may follow this pattern, layered upon – rather than replacing – existing regimes.

We have also identified a number of relationships whose characterisation will ultimately depend on the way in which the account holders interpret their powers and choose to exercise them. This seems to apply to two roles in particular: first to that of Secretary of State, who has potentially significant powers over the NHS Commissioning Board and consortia but has committed politically to less central intervention in the service; and second to that of the NHS Commissioning Board – its choice of a lighter or heavier approach to performance management when performance assessing consortia will have a significant influence on the culture of the system as a whole.

Conclusions

The reforms set out in *Equity and Excellence: Liberating the NHS* (Department of Health 2010a) and the Health and Social Care Bill (House of Commons 2010–11) will, if implemented, significantly change the structures and processes by which commissioners and providers of NHS care are held to account. Many of the existing institutions that currently play a role in holding parts of the system to account would be abolished. There is also a commitment, at least in theory, to enhance local accountability and reduce central control, in an effort to make the NHS more accountable to patients.

So what will the changes analysed in this paper mean for how accountability operates in the health system?

Secondary care providers

For secondary care providers, the changes mean a greater reliance on regulation, internal governance and transparency. These types of relationships are very different from the direct managerial accountability that they replace. Some commentators have questioned whether they constitute accountability at all. Although information and transparency are a prerequisite for accountability, they do not in themselves make an organisation accountable as they do not require it to explain its conduct.

The internal governance arrangements of an organisation would also fall outside of some definitions of accountability as there is no independent, external account holder. On the other hand, it can be argued that robust internal governance arrangements, which include, for example, independent appointees, may reduce the need for strong external accountability. The external accountabilities of foundation trusts will be weaker in future as the new Monitor will no longer monitor their performance post-authorisation, thus placing a greater reliance on governors. We have questioned whether the broadening of governors' scope will actually strengthen their hand in relation to the board, given experiences with this model to date.

Regulation is often also excluded from accounts of public accountability because the activities of regulators are restricted to monitoring compliance with an explicit and circumscribed set of standards. Regulators cannot call organisations to account for their behaviour; they can only judge whether to license an organisation and whether to exercise a narrow set of sanctions if standards are not being met. Regulation also offers assurances only in relation to minimum standards of safety and quality.

The accountability of secondary care providers for providing a good or excellent service in the new system will therefore depend heavily on commissioners, whose effectiveness is likely to vary considerably at a local level. The recent history of the NHS suggests that commissioners are relatively ineffective in holding powerful providers to account (House of Commons Health Committee 2010a), and it is difficult to see why or how this might be different under the new system, particularly in the short to medium term as consortia establish themselves.

Given this, we are concerned that the accountability of secondary care providers will be underpowered, which would result in potentially significant local variation in the quality and value for money of secondary care services. In this context, the role of boards in holding organisations to account for improving the quality of services will take on a new importance, and work to support and strengthen the capacity of board members to do this effectively ought to be given renewed attention.

GP practices

GP practices as providers would see a significant increase in the accountability requirements placed on them, including a new relationship with the GP commissioning consortia of which they are members. Other new requirements to account to Monitor, the Care Quality Commission, the NHS Commissioning Board and local authorities will be particularly demanding for small and single-handed practices. As The King's Fund's inquiry into the quality of general practice concluded (The King's Fund 2011b), smaller practices will be better placed to manage such demands if they join larger networks or organisations.

Commissioners

In contrast to secondary care providers, managerial and political accountability will continue for GP commissioners who are responsible for spending public money. Although the relationship between the NHS Commissioning Board and GP consortia is described by the Government as quasi-regulatory, the NHS Commissioning Board has potentially wide-ranging powers of intervention in relation to consortia. The 'authorisation' regime that the NHS Commissioning Board will operate for consortia may be relatively weak in its infancy, as it will be difficult for consortia to demonstrate their ability to perform tasks that they have not performed before. Furthermore, the internal governance arrangements for GP consortia are currently less demanding and more opaque than those of the primary care trusts they replace, and health and wellbeing boards lack sufficient powers to hold consortia to account. In this context, the NHS Commissioning Board may well have good reason to play a strongly interventionist role in relation to consortia.

Mandating and supporting consortia to develop robust and transparent governance arrangements would reduce the need for NHS Commissioning Board intervention. Given that consortia pathfinders are already establishing their organisational form, the government should attend to this as a matter of urgency. Health and wellbeing boards should also be given more power to hold consortia to account for securing services that meet the health needs of the local population. The requirement on the NHS Commissioning Board to take account of the views of local health and wellbeing boards should be strengthened.

Overall conclusions

It is difficult to produce an overall assessment of whether the reforms will mean that the health service is more or less accountable. Health systems have multiple and often competing objectives – equity of access, value for money, clinical effectiveness and so on. Different accountability mechanisms may be more effective at holding organisations to account for some of these values and not others. In this context, combining different types of accountability mechanisms – scrutiny, contractual, etc – is almost certainly appropriate as long as care is taken to avoid overlaps, gaps and overly burdensome requirements on organisations, and that there is clarity across the system regarding the range of accountability relationships. However, judging which blend of mechanisms produces the better system of accountability depends on which values are prioritised.

The government has been keen to emphasise the negative aspects of managerial and political accountability. The dismantling of managerial accountability (at least for providers) is justified by the government as necessary for rebalancing the overall system of accountability to one in which organisations are more responsive to the patients they serve rather than to targets and guidance from the centre. The Bill includes measures to reduce political interference, although it is not clear whether the changes to the powers of the Secretary of State will prevent a future incumbent with more interventionist tendencies from exercising these powers.

We have raised doubts about the strength of local accountability mechanisms for both providers and commissioners and conclude that, overall, the reforms signal a shift to a system that is overly reliant on local mechanisms, which are at best unproven in their efficacy.

Past experience tells us that informal relationships between organisations and individuals will play a significant part in characterising the new accountability regime (Storey *et al* 2010). The legislative framework set out in the Health and Social Care Bill is quite permissive, leaving much of the detail to secondary legislation and subsequent guidance, or local determination. The reduced role of central direction and the requirements on organisations within the system to pay regard to each other in a mutually co-operative manner mean that informal relationships will be even more important in the future. How these relationships are acted out by the people who occupy key positions within the new system will ultimately determine who has the power and who, in fact, is accountable to whom and for what. It may not be as easy to follow the traditional formal lines of accountability in the future. Whether such complexity reduces the effectiveness of accountability remains to be seen, but we suspect it might.

In this paper we have focused on the immediate accountability relationships for providers and commissioners of NHS care. However, the onward chain of these relationships involves a strong link between the managerial accountability that is so dominant in the current system, with political accountability of the NHS through the Secretary of State to parliament. The Health and Social Care Bill sets out a new framework of accountability for the NHS, one in which the market, regulation and local scrutiny will all play a much greater role, and managerial and political accountability for secondary care providers will play a commensurately smaller one.

Yet the NHS remains one of the largest domains of public expenditure, and in a tighter fiscal environment with increasing pressures on budgets there will continue to be demands for political accountability, both about how the money is being spent and for how local services are provided, particularly where there are closures. The dismantling of lines of managerial and political accountability might make it more difficult for elected politicians in Westminster to get a clear account in future, but they will no doubt try. Systems of contractual accountability and oversight by local democratic bodies may not be sufficient to satisfy their demands. Whatever the government's intentions, we may yet see a resurgence of central managerial and political accountability for providers as well as commissioners of NHS care.

References

Addicott R (2005). *Power, Governance and Knowledge: The example of London managed clinical networks for cancer.* Tanaka Business School. London: Imperial College London. PhD.

Audit Commission/Healthcare Commission (2008). *Is the Treatment Working? Progress with the NHS system reform programme.* London: Audit Commission. Available at: www.audit-commission.gov.uk/SiteCollectionDocuments/ AuditCommissionReports/NationalStudies/IstheTreatmentWorking.pdf (accessed on 4 April 2011).

Bovens M (2006). *Analysing and Assessing Public Accountability. A conceptual framework.* European Governance Paper (EUROGOV) no C-06-01. Available at: www.connex-network.org/eurogov/pdf/egp-connex-C-06-01.pdf (accessed on 4 April 2011).

Boyce T, Dixon A, Fasolo B, Reutskaja E (2010). *Choosing a High-Quality Hospital: The role of nudges, scorecard design and information.* London: The King's Fund. Available at: www.kingsfund.org.uk/publications/choosing_a.html (accessed on 4 April 2011).

Brereton L, Gubb J (2010). *Refusing Treatment: The NHS and market-based reform.* London: CIVITAS: Institute for the Study of Civil Society. Available at: www.civitas.org.uk/nhs/pubs_articles.php (accessed on 23 February 2011).

Carvel J (2008). 'NHS chief accused of eroding hospitals' independence'. *Guardian,* 19 February 2008.

Coleman A, Gains F, Boyd A, Bradshaw D, Johnson C (2009). 'Scrutinising local public service provision: lessons from the experience of health scrutiny 2004–2007'. *Public Money and Management,* pp 299–306.

Curry N, Goodwin N, Naylor C, Robertson R (2008). *Practice-based Commissioning: Reinvigorate, replace or abandon?.* London: The King's Fund. Available at: www.kingsfund.org.uk/publications/pbc.html (accessed on 4 April 2011).

Day P, Klein R (2005). *Governance of Foundation Trusts: Dilemmas of diversity.* London: Nuffield Trust. Available at: www.nuffieldtrust.org.uk/ecomm/files/ 100605governance.pdf (accessed on 11 April 2011)

Day P, Klein R (1987). *Accountabilities: Five public services.* London: Tavistock Publications.

Department of Health (2010a). *Equity and Excellence: Liberating the NHS.* Cm 7881. London: The Stationery Office. Available at: www.dh.gov.uk/en/ Publicationsandstatistics/Publications/PublicationsPolicyAndGuidance/ DH_117353 (accessed on 4 April 2011).

Department of Health (2010b). *Healthy Lives, Healthy People: Our strategy for public health in England* [online]. Available at: www.dh.gov.uk/en/ Publicationsandstatistics/Publications/PublicationsPolicyAndGuidance/ DH_121941 (accessed on 4 April 2011).

Department of Health (2010c). *Liberating the NHS: Commissioning for patients – consultation on proposals* [online]. Available at: www.dh.gov.uk/en/Consultations/ Liveconsultations/DH_117587 (accessed on 4 April 2011).

Department of Health (2010d). *Liberating the NHS: Increasing democratic legitimacy in health* [online]. Available at: www.dh.gov.uk/en/Consultations/ Liveconsultations/DH_117586 (accessed on 4 April 2011).

Department of Health (2010e). *Liberating the NHS: Legislative framework and next steps.* Cm 7993. London: The Stationery Office. *Available at:* www.dh.gov. uk/prod_consum_dh/groups/dh_digitalassets/@dh/@en/@ps/documents/ digitalasset/dh_122707.pdf (accessed on 4 April 2011).

Department of Health (2010f). *Liberating the NHS: Regulating healthcare providers* [online]. Available at: www.dh.gov.uk/prod_consum_dh/groups/ dh_digitalassets/@dh/@en/documents/digitalasset/dh_117842.pdf (accessed on 4 April 2011).

Department of Health (2010g). *Local Involvement Networks (LINks) Annual Reports 2009/10* [online]. Available at: www.dh.gov.uk/en/ Publicationsandstatistics/Publications/PublicationsPolicyAndGuidance/ DH_123155 (accessed on 4 April 2011).

Department of Health (2010h). *The Operating Framework for the NHS in England 2011/12.* London: Department of Health. Available at: www.dh.gov.uk/prod_ consum_dh/groups/dh_digitalassets/@dh/@en/@ps/documents/digitalasset/ dh_122736.pdf (accessed on 7 April 2011).

Department of Health (2010i). *Written Evidence from Experts in Severe and Complex Obesity (COM 108)* [online]. Paragraph 12. Available at: www. publications.parliament.uk/pa/cm201011/cmselect/cmhealth/513/513vw103.htm (accessed on 7 April 2011).

Department of Health (2003a). *Governing the NHS: A guide for NHS boards.* London: Department of Health. Available at: www.dh.gov.uk/en/Publicationsandstatistics/ Publications/PublicationsPolicyAndGuidance/DH_4082638 (accessed on 13 April 2011).

Department of Health (2003b). *Overview and Scrutiny of Health – Guidance*. London: Department of Health. Available at: www.dh.gov.uk/en/ Publicationsandstatistics/Publications/PublicationsLegislation/DH_4009607 (accessed on 4 April 2011).

Department of Health and NHS Appointments Commission (2004). *Code of Conduct. Code of accountability in the NHS* [online]. Available at: www.dh.gov. uk/en/Publicationsandstatistics/Publications/PublicationsPolicyAndGuidance/ DH_4116281 (accessed on 12 April 2011).

Dixon A, Storey J, Rosete A (2010a). 'Accountability of foundation trusts in the English NHS: views of directors and governors'. *Journal of Health Services Research & Policy*, vol 15, no 2, pp 82–9.

Dixon A, Robertson, R, Appleby J, Burge P, Devlin N, Magee H (2010b). *Patient Choice: How patients choose and how providers respond*. London: The King's Fund. Available at: www.kingsfund.org.uk/publications/patient_choice.html (accessed on 22 February 2011).

Exworthy M, Frosini F, Peckham S, Powell M, Greener I, Holloway JA (2009). *Decentralisation and Performance: Autonomy and incentives in local health economies*. Southampton: National Co-ordinating Centre for the NHS Service Delivery and Organisation (NCCSDO) R&D.

Fisher ES, Shortell SM (2010). 'Accountable care organizations. Accountable for what, to whom, and how?'. *Journal of the American Medical Association*, vol 304, no 15, pp 1715–16.

Foot C, Raleigh V, Ross S, Lyscom T (2011). *How Do Quality Accounts Measure Up? Findings from the first year*. London: The King's Fund. Available at: www. kingsfund.org.uk/publications/quality_accounts_1.html (accessed on 4 April 2011).

Ham C (2011). 'Competition in the NHS in England'. *British Medical Journal*, vol 342, no d1035, p 395.

Ham C, Hunt P (2008). *Membership Governance in NHS Foundation Trusts: A review for the Department of Health* [online]. Elstree and Birmingham: Mutuo and the University of Birmingham. Available at: www.dh.gov.uk/en/ Publicationsandstatistics/Publications/PublicationsPolicyAndGuidance/ DH_086374 (accessed on 4 April 2011).

Hansard (2010a). *Hansard (House of Commons Debates)* (2010–11) 16 November 2010 col 41WS. Available at: www.publications.parliament.uk/pa/cm201011/ cmhansrd/cm101116/wmstext/101116m0001.htm (accessed on 4 April 2011).

Hansard (2010b). *Hansard (House of Lords Debates)* (2010–11) 13 December 2010 col c130W. Available at: http://services.parliament.uk/hansard/Lords/ByDate/20101213/writtenanswers/part039.html (accessed on 4 April 2011).

Healthcare Commission (2005). *The Healthcare Commission's Review of NHS Foundation Trusts.* London: Healthcare Commission. Available at: www.cqc.org.uk/_db/_documents/4815-Foundation_Trusts-v10.pdf (accessed on 4 April 2011).

Her Majesty's Government (2010). *The Coalition: Our programme for government.* London: The Cabinet Office. Available at: www.cabinetoffice.gov.uk/sites/default/files/resources/coalition_programme_for_government.pdf (accessed on 4 April 2011).

Her Majesty's Government (2006) *National Health Service Act 2006,* chapter 41. London: The Stationery Office. Available at: www.legislation.gov.uk/ukpga/2006/41/contents (accessed on 4 April 2011).

Hibbard JH, Jewett JJ (1997). 'Will quality report cards help consumers?'. *Health Affairs,* vol 16, no 3, pp 218–28. Available at: http://content.healthaffairs.org/content/16/3/218.full.pdf (accessed on 4 April 2011).

Hood C, James O, Scott C (2000). 'Regulation of government: has it increased, is it increasing, should it be diminished?'. *Public Administration,* vol 78, no 2, pp 283–304. Available at: http://people.exeter.ac.uk/ojames/pubadmin2000vol78no2hoodjamesscottreginsidegovt.pdf (accessed on 4 April 2011).

House of Commons (2011). *Health and Social Care Bill Explanatory Notes.* HCB 132–EN. London: The Stationery Office. Available at: www.publications.parliament.uk/pa/cm201011/cmbills/132/en/11132en.pdf (accessed on 4 April 2011).

House of Commons Bill (2010–11). 132. *Health and Social Care Bill* [online]. Available at: www.publications.parliament.uk/pa/cm201011/cmbills/132/11132.i-v.html (accessed on 4 April 2011).

House of Commons Health Committee (2010a). *Commissioning. Fourth Report of Session 2009–10. HC 268-I.* London: The Stationery Office. Available at: www.publications.parliament.uk/pa/cm200910/cmselect/cmhealth/268/268i.pdf (accessed on 4 April 2011).

House of Commons Health Committee (2010b). *Oral Evidence Taken before the Health Committee,* Tuesday 23 November [online]. Available at: www.publications.parliament.uk/pa/cm201011/cmselect/cmhealth/512/10112301.htm (accessed on 11 April 2011).

Klein R, New B (1998). *Two Cheers? Reflections on the health of NHS democracy.* London: The King's Fund.

Lewis R (2005). *Governing Foundation Trusts: A new era for public accountability.* London: The King's Fund. Available at: www.kingsfund.org.uk/publications/governing.html (accessed on 4 April 2011).

Lewis R, Hinton L (2008). 'Citizen and staff involvement in health service decision-making: have National Health Service foundation trusts in England given stakeholders a louder voice?'. *Journal of Health Services Research*, vol 13, no 1, pp 19–25.

Likierman A (2006). 'Seven questions to assess your non-executives'. *Health Service Journal*, 6 November 2006. Available at: http://www.hsj.co.uk/resource-centre/seven-questions-to-assess-your-non-executives/3152.article (accessed on 12 April 2011).

Mulgan R (2003). *Holding Power to Account. Accountability in modern democracies.* New York: MacMillan Palgrave.

Mulgan R (2000). '"Accountability": an ever-expanding concept?'. *Public Administration*, vol 78, no 3, pp 555–73.

NHS Confederation and Independent Healthcare Advisory Services (2009). *What's It All For? Removing unnecessary bureaucracy in regulation.* London: NHS Confederation and Independent Healthcare Advisory Services. Available at: www.nhsconfed.org/Publications/Documents/Whats_it_all_for.pdf (accessed on 4 April 2011).

Nicholson D (2011). 'Equity and Excellence: Liberating the NHS - managing the transition'. Dear Colleague Letter [online]. Department of Health website. Available at: www.dh.gov.uk/en/Publicationsandstatistics/Lettersandcirculars/Dearcolleagueletters/DH_124440 (accessed on 11 April 2011).

Sinclair A (1995). 'The chameleon of accountability: forms and discourses'. *Accounting, Organizations and Society*, vol 20, no 2/3, pp 219–37.

Storey J, Holti R, Winchester N, Green R, Salaman G, Bate P (2010). *The Intended and Unintended Outcomes of New Governance Arrangements within the NHS.* Southampton: National Co-ordinating Centre for the NHS Service Delivery and Organisation (NCCSDO). Available at: www.sdo.nihr.ac.uk/files/project/SDO_FR_08-1618-129_V01.pdf (accessed on 4 April 2011).

The King's Fund (2011a). *Consultation Response: Liberating the NHS: An information revolution* [online]. Available at: www.kingsfund.org.uk/document.rm?id=8931 (accessed on 4 April 2011).

The King's Fund (2011b). *Improving the Quality of Care in General Practice. Report of an independent inquiry commissioned by The King's Fund.* London: The King's Fund. Available at: www.kingsfund.org.uk/publications/gp_inquiry_report.html (accessed on 13 April 2011).

Thorlby R, Lewis R, Dixon J (2008). *Should Primary Care Trusts Be Made More Locally Accountable?* London: The King's Fund. Available at: www.kingsfund.org.uk/publications/local_accountability.html (accessed on 4 April 2011).

Tuohy CH (2003). 'Agency, contract and governance: shifting shapes of accountability in the health care arena'. *Journal of Health Politics, Policy and Law*, vol 28, no 2–3, pp 195–216.